LOVE AND THE LAW

A PRONOMIAN POCKET GUIDE TO JOHN 14:15

BENJAMIN SZUMSKYJ

Love and the Law: A Pronomian Pocket Guide to John 14:15

Copyright © 2025 Benjamin Szumskyj. All rights reserved.

Pronomian Publishing LLC
Clover, SC 29710

ISBN: 979-8-9908630-4-0

Publisher grants permission to reference short quotations (fewer than 300 words) in reviews, magazines, newspapers, websites, or other publications. Request for permission to reproduce more than 300 words can be made at **www.pronomianpublishing.com/contact**

Scripture quotations taken from the (NASB®) New American Standard Bible®, Copyright © 1960, 1971, 1977, 1995 by The Lockman Foundation. Used by permission. All rights reserved. lockman.org.

Dr. Benjamin Szumskyj's *Love and the Law: A Pronomian Pocket Guide to John 14:15* is a compelling contribution to the ongoing discussion of the continuity of the Torah's commandments in the life of believers. With clarity and precision, Szumskyj offers a robust, historically grounded exegesis of Jesus' words; "If you love Me, you will keep My commandments," challenging contemporary interpretations that often separate love from obedience. Through his pronomian stance, he compellingly argues for the enduring relevance of the Torah's commandments, presenting love not as a passive sentiment but as a call to active, faithful living in accordance with God's Word. Balancing scholarly depth with accessible language, this concise yet impactful work is a valuable resource for both lay readers and scholars seeking to deepen their understanding of John 14:15 and its practical implications for Christian discipleship. I will certainly be using the book with my students.

—Julie O'Toole, Wellington Pacific Bible College

Dr. Benjamin Szumskyj's "pocket guide" is a robust commentary on the Scripture, John 14:15, where he views the relationship of love toward God as an expression of keeping the commandments as the aim of the book. In expounding on the meaning of *entolē* (ἐντολή), he draws on a large periphery of biblical themes. This further clarifies Messianic scholar Tim Hegg's explanation that the term "commandments" refers to the unity of Scripture, as reflected by the Hebrew word *mitzvah* (מִצְוָה) in the singular, which encompasses the entire body of law. The book offers a Pronomian interpretation supported by Karen Jobes, where the first part of the verse is a third-class conditional in the present imperfective, followed by an unusual use of the future active indicative in the second part of the verse (instead of the imperative that would be expected). All this is to mean that there is a preference for *tērēsete* rather than *tērēsate* (keep, observe, guard, obey to mean an imperative (τηρήσατε in a majority of MSS) with a hint of promise, or as Benjamin would put it, "an obedient love" where obedience to Torah is geared to one's love to Messiah and to "one another" in the community of the church (ἐκκλησία). Benjamin, in his inimitable style, navigates freely through connected themes with a multiplicity of Scriptures. An invaluable part of this commentary is its robust use of references, which also provide a heuristic for further study to both students and teachers.

—Pj de Marigny, Talbot School of Theology

Dedicated to Walter C. Kaiser Jr.

CONTENTS

Foreword 1

Introduction 3

1. Understanding the "new commandment" in John 13:34 11

2. An Exegesis of John 14:15 17

3. Parallel Passages in Johannine Literature 37

4. A Pronomian Interpretation of John 14:15 47

5. Doing the Commandments as a Community 57

Conclusion 77

Appendix 1: The Role of Godly Works in the Markan Shema 81

Appendix 2: God is Light (1 John 1:5–10) 89

Appendix 3: The Gospel of Messiah Yeshua 99

Postscript 103

Bibliography 105

FOREWORD

People often say that good things sometimes come in small packages. That is not always the case, but it certainly holds true for this book by Dr. Benjamin Szumskyj.

Love and the Law: A Pronomian Pocket Guide to John 14:15 is an extended exposition of John 14:15 where Dr. Szumskyj explores in rather great detail what Yeshua meant when He taught "If you love Me, you will keep My commandments." A plethora of sermons and biblical expositions have been produced about this famous passage over the course of centuries. However, very seldom—if at all—has a study even been made that upholds the veracity and authority of the Torah of Moshe, the written revelation the Holy One gave Moshe at Mt. Sinai.

All too often Yeshua's "commandments" are understood in contrast to those of Moshe's writings. Dr. Szumskyj carefully explains how such a contradiction is not only contrived but absurd, inadvertently resulting in the Scripture actually contradicting itself. Dr. Szumskyj upholds the integrity of Scripture by eliminating any such possible contradiction between the written Torah and the teaching of the Living Torah, Yeshua.

In addition to a careful exposition of John 14:15, Dr. Szumskyj also covers his bases! He anticipates possible objections from possible detractors by abundantly supporting his assertions with an assortment of quotations and ideas from other scholars on the subject. This adds much credibility to Szumskyj's position of upholding the Torah. Furthermore, it shows that there are other scholarly and spiritual believers who are beginning to think alike concerning the role of Torah in the life of one who trusts in Yeshua.

Thus, it is with great enthusiasm that I commend this brief study to the reader and student of Scripture. You will be challenged and blessed at the same time. Moreover, I am certain that this volume will be a useful addition to the growing amount of literature supporting the new phenomena called "pronomianism."

—Ariel Berkowitz
Arad, Israel

INTRODUCTION

What does it mean to love Yeshua?[1] The apostle John records Yeshua's own answer to this question in John 14:15. Yeshua said, "If you love Me, you will keep My commandments." The connection between "love" and "commandments" is a major theme in John's Gospel. But what are these commandments that Yeshua refers to? Do they come from the Law of Moses (Torah), or are they something entirely new? This book explores how John's Gospel answers these questions and what Yeshua's words mean for believers today who seek to love him.

Who Was John?

Before we dive into the connection between "love" and "law," let us first take a moment to learn about John, who authored the Fourth Gospel between 85–90 AD. Along with his older brother James ("the sons of Zebedee," Mark 3:17; Matt. 10:2), John was a Galilean fisherman and personally called to be among Messiah Yeshua's twelve apostles. John is often referred to as the one whom Yeshua "loved" (John 13:23, 20:2, 21:7, 21:20), one of three whom were a part of Yeshua's inner circle (Matt. 17:1; 26:37), and in order to magnify the Messiah, he humbly wrote about himself in the third person (John 13:23, 19:26, 20:2, 21:7, 20). John's insight into the life and teachings of Yeshua were intimate (cf. 1 John 1:1–4), and he was well versed in ancient Hebrew and Greek, strengthening the historical understanding that he died as a proficient pastor-teacher in Ephesus.[2] He was one

---

1 Unless citing from Scripture or a source, I will refer to Jesus by his Hebrew name, Yeshua.
2 An excellent starting point on the Greek Scriptures is D. Edmond Heibert, *An*

of the most prolific authors in the Greek Scriptures (New Testament), accredited with writing the Gospel of John, 1 John, 2 John, 3 John, and Revelation. A little-known fact to many readers is that John the apostle may have been the cousin of Yeshua. In Matthew 27:56, the mother of John and James is mentioned anonymously, but when read in tangent with Mark 15:40 and John 19:25, it appears that her name was Salome the sister of Mary, Yeshua's mother.

The Gospel according to John, the last of the four biographical gospels, offers a more personal and theological interpretation of the Messiah's life and ministry, rather than a strictly historical account. It is an exploration of Yeshua that explicitly emphasizes the doctrine of the Messiah, for "it is *eternal life* that is the key theme to express what in the Synoptics is the kingdom promise... [and it] is the *Word/Logos* sent from God in the form of human flesh that brings this promise," so much that "the role of signs for John is crucial [as he] focuses on acts of healing, restoration, and provision... [in order that] Jesus is seen as the *Revelator* of God [and] makes the Father and his way known."[3] John's goal with his account was not just to explore the humanity of God the Son, but to expound his divine nature with God the Father. Yeshua is depicted as the means of establishing a relationship with YHWH, in which believers will be eternally rewarded if they are to accept the truth of his words and message of salvation. Yeshua is the Word made flesh, who gives the words of life and lives in perfect accordance with those

---

Introduction to the New Testament: Three Volume Collection (Waynesboro, GA: Gabriel Publishing, 2003) and D.A. Carson and Douglas J. Moo, *An Introduction to the New Testament* (Grand Rapids: Zondervan, 2005).

3 Darrell L. Bock, *Studying the Historical Jesus: A Guide to Sources and Methods* (Grand Rapids: Baker Book House Company, 2002), 34.

very holy words he delivered as one member of the Tri-Unity at Mt. Sinai, marking the birth of the ecclesia.[4]

Like the other gospels, the Gospel of John has traditionally been understood as addressed primarily to a specific community. Bauckman, however, pushes against the idea that each written gospel account was exclusively for a specific type of audience.[5] Regardless of whether or not the authors wrote first for specific communities, it seems clear that "they wrote for any and every church to which their Gospels might circulate."[6]

---

4   See Tim Hegg, *I Will Build My Ekklesia: An Introduction to Ecclesiology* (Tacoma, WA: Torah Resource, 2009) and Benjamin Szumskyj, "Chapters 4: The Israel of God and the Ecclesia as One: Covenantally Living out the Torah," in *The Laws of Torah in the Sanctification of the Modern Christian: A Brief Introduction to Pronomianism* (Wilmington, DE: Vernon Press, 2026). For a similar conclusion, see R. L. Watson, *Forgotten Covenant* (New South Wales, Australia: Ark Press, 2021), 316–326.

5   Bauckman contends the "antecedent probability that someone writing a Gospel in the late first century would have envisaged the kind of general Christian audience which the Gospels in fact very soon achieved through circulation around the churches." He notes that "mobility and communication in the first-century Roman world were exceptionally high," that "the early Christian movement had a strong sense of itself as a worldwide movement," that "Christian leaders of whom we know in the New Testament period moved around," the "continuous practice from the time of Paul to the mid-second century is the sending of letters from one church to another," that "concrete evidence for close contacts between churches in the period around or soon after the writing of the Gospels," and "evidence for conflict and diversity in early Christianity [reveals] the early Christian movement as a network of communities in constant communication." See Richard Bauckham, "For Whom Were Gospels Written?," in *The Gospels for All Christians: Rethinking the Gospel Audiences*, ed. Richard Bauckham (Grand Rapids: William B. Eerdmans Publishing Company, 1998), 26, 32–33, 38–39, 43, 46. Whether he was aware of Bauckham's work or not, Hengel came to a similar conclusion. Martin Hengel, *The Four Gospels and the One Gospel of Jesus Christ*, trans. J. Bowden (London: SCM Press, 2000), 107.

6   Bauckham, "For Whom Were Gospels Written?," 46.

Introduction

Love and the Law

As mentioned previously, a key theme in the Gospel of John is the author's emphasis on the importance of works as a result of salvation—the fruit of being born again. Most striking is the connection between "love" and "commandments." In John 14:15 we read, "If you love me, you will keep my commandments." This is a confronting statement, for our contemporary understanding of love does not naturally associate itself with observing anything commanded of us. However, Leon Morris rightly notes the following:

> In modern times we often confuse love with sentimentality, and we do not always see as clearly as the prophets did that there is a stern side to real love. Any easy sentimentality will decline to take stern action when the beloved does what is wrong. But this leaves the beloved secure in his wrongdoing, unfairly confirming the very action that makes him less of a person. Because sentimentality refuses to do what is distasteful, it ignores the long-term benefits of reproving the beloved because it sees that he will dislike the immediate unpleasantness. Sentimentality thus takes the easy way out. But the more one loves, the more one hates the things that present the beloved from enjoying the fullest and most abundant life.[7]

It is my contention that if we truly love YHWH,[8] through Yeshua the Messiah, that we will lovingly keep his commandments and not

---

[7] Leon Morris, *Testaments of Love: A Study of Love in the Bible* (Grand Rapids: William B. Eerdmans, 1981), 25. This work is one of the finest treatments on biblical love ever published.

[8] Unless contextually unnecessary or citing another's work, I will refer to the God of Israel by his personal name, YHWH (יהוה).

hate anything he has commanded. The contention of this book, then, is that love of Yeshua is evidenced in the life of a believer by living out the commandments, for an unchanging God and his unchanging attribute of holiness is the standard by which his commands are established.

What are the "Commandments"?

Church history is full of interpretations, some of which are more popular than others. Space does not allow for a thorough examination of the Gospel of John's interpretive history. However, a solid reading of various volumes highlights that there are three consistent interpretations of John 14:15, the foundational text studied in this book. The first interpretation is that the laws referred to by Messiah Yeshua in John 14:15 are those he taught during his earthly ministry, forming the basis of the Greek Scriptures (New Testament), rather than the commandments found in the Hebrew Scriptures (Old Testament). This is the dominant view, shaped by the theological position that from his conception to his death, Yeshua fulfilled the Torah in such a way that rendered it inoperative, with only the "moral laws" and those repeated in the Greek Scriptures remaining. As Colin Kruse states, "Love for Jesus is not sentimental, but is expressed by keeping his commands, i.e. by responding to all he taught, with faith and obedience… [and i]n other passages Jesus' teaching is described as his word (*logos*), referring to his teaching as a whole."[9] J. C. Ryle adds the following:

---

9   Colin G. Kruse, *John: An Introduction and Commentary* (Downers Grove, IL: InterVarsity Press, 2003), 299.

> Let us notice how our Lord speaks of 'my commandments.'
> We never read of Moses or any other servant of God using
> such an expression. It is the language of one who was one
> with God the Father, and had power to lay down laws and
> make statutes for his church.[10]

A variation of this view holds that during Yeshua's earthly ministry, his statement in John 14:15 did refer to laws from both the Hebrew and Greek Scriptures. However, after his death and resurrection, it now only pertains to the Greek Scriptures.

The second interpretation is that John 14:15 pertains to the main commandments of the previous chapters, namely, to receive (and respond to) the love of YHWH and to love others. Frederick Bruner articulates this position:

> There have been two special commands of Jesus to his
> disciples here in his Discipleship Sermons so far: (a) first of
> all, to let themselves be loved (to be washed clean) by the
> Lord (13:8)—or what is the same thing (and this has been the
> most repeated command in Jesus' Father Sermon so far)—to
> believe into Jesus (see esp. 14:1 and 11 for this believe/trust/
> entrust command and plea). And then, out of this resource of
> being loved, out of this well of believed belovedness, comes
> immediately and almost spontaneously another command
> or direction, (b) to love one another, to wash one another's

---

[10] J. C. Ryle, *John – Volume 3: Expository Thoughts on the Gospels* (Edinburgh, UK: The Banner of Truth Trust, 2012), 54. This statement implies a disconnect in realizing that all three persons of the Tri-Unity delivered the commandments to Moses on Mt. Sinai, which is when the ecclesia was established.

feet in the Church and in the world, especially for the sake of Jesus' world mission.[11]

Last, the minority view is the interpretation that Yeshua is referring to the totality of the Torah, which is to be understood as those in the Hebrew Scriptures and enlarged by the Greek Scriptures.[12] This pro-Torah hermeneutic is known as "One Law" theology or pronomianism.[13]

It is this last view that will shape *Love and the Law*. As mentioned earlier, the nature and parameters of holiness as established and evidenced by YHWH are unchanging. The commandment that was holy and brought him glory yesterday cannot be declared as no longer holy today (or even unholy as some have preached). While there are denominations that contend the laws of the Torah are no longer relevant today, but insist that these commandments will be relevant to the redeemed Jew in Messiah during the eschatological Millenium, this is grossly inconsistent. It must then be conceded that, if the commandments as established in accordance with the holiness of YHWH were

---

11 Frederick Dale Bruner, *The Gospel of John: A Commentary* (Grand Rapids, MI: William B. Eerdmans, 2012), 80. See also Victor Paul Furnish, *The Love Command in the New Testament* (London, UK: SCM Press, 1973), 137.

12 Jer. 31:33; 1 Cor. 14:21; 1 Tim. 5:17–18; cf. John 10:34; 12:34.

13 Benjamin Szumskyj, *The Laws of Torah in the Sanctification of the Modern Christian: A Brief Introduction to Pronomianism* (Wilmington, DE: Vernon Press, 2026). In my book, I propose that the Torah can be applied today in two ways: a) literally, meaning that what has been written can be applied in any culture or environment and is not bound by time, due to its straightforward understanding and ability to be practised, and b) non-literally, meaning that it cannot be applied directly due to a temporary suspension enacted by YHWH (i.e., the Levitical priesthood) or the absence of a component dependent on the commandment being fulfilled as is (e.g., the physical Temple), demanding a principle or paradigm to be extracted and applied. This model is not a new creation, but rather, evidenced by Scripture itself. For example, there are times when the apostle Paul literally applied the laws of the Torah (Acts 21:17–24; Gal. 5:3), and there are times in which he did so by way of principle (1 Tim. 5:17–18).

Introduction

true for thousands of years prior to the incarnation of Yeshua, comprising the Torah, then they must remain so "until heaven and earth pass away, [for] not the smallest letter or stroke shall pass from the Law [i.e. Torah] until all is accomplished" (Matt. 5:18). Love and obedience have always been as one throughout the scriptural record (Deut. 7:7, 10:12-13). John 14:15 teaches that commandment-observance is an ongoing reality in the sanctification of the believer and serves as a demonstration of love—a love expected of *all* believers (Matt. 22:34–40; 1 John 4:7-21). We do not hate Yeshua, rejecting his commandments, but love him, and do his commandments. It is time for a second Reformation, one that restores the full light of the lamp to our feet and the light to our path (Psalm 119:105).

Soli Deo Gloria and Tota Scriptura
Dr. Benjamin Szumskyj, 2025

CHAPTER 1
UNDERSTANDING THE "NEW COMMANDMENT" IN JOHN 13:34

In John 13:34, Yeshua tells his disciples that he has given them "a new commandment" to "love one another, even as I have loved you." Since the interpretation of this verse influences how we understand John 14:15 and the role of the Torah in the lives of believers, we must it address it early. Is Messiah Yeshua's "new" commandment *entirely new*, replacing those delivered to the prophet Moses and shaping all relevant verses in the Johannine literature regarding love and commandment observance? Or does this verse present an enlarged and renewed understanding of love as established by YHWH in the Torah, affirming the continuity of his commanded instructions from the Mosaic era to believers today?

There are two main schools of thought. The first possible interpretation is that this is a totally new commandment that has no connection to the previous commandments in the Hebrew Scriptures and, in fact, replaces them.[1] As William MacDonald succinctly puts it, "The commandments of the Lord are the instructions which He has given us in the Gospels, as well as the rest of the NT."[2] This interpretation contends that verses such as John 14:15 are not about the Torah, but solely regarding the "new" commandment of love referred to by Yeshua

---

1 Lawrence O. Richards, "Command/Commandments," in *Expository Dictionary of Bible Words* (Grand Rapids: Zondervan, 1985), 178.
2 William MacDonald, *Believer's Bible Commentary* (Nashville: Thomas Nelson, 1995), 1547; Colin G. Kruse, *The Letters of John: The Pillar New Testament Commentary* (Grand Rapids: William B. Eerdmans, 2000), 78–79.

in the passage, different from any definition and standard of love as prescribed by YHWH in the past. Graystone echoes MacDonald's perspective:

> [W]herein lies the newness of the commandment? (i) In the Gospel and 1 John there is no other commandment (cf. 15:12). The love commandment displaces all others, not because other commandments are unnecessary for promoting justice and happiness in social life, but because 'We have crossed over from death to life, because we love our fellow Christians' (1 John 3:14). This is the commandment, beyond all others, which permits those in this world to experience the life of the heavenly world. (ii) It is not simply a commandment of mutual love but love as I have loved you. Jesus loved as the Agent of the Father's love, and he carried that love to the point of death knowing that death took him to life with the Father. So the new commandment is that his disciples love as agents of the Father's love, and give themselves without reserve to the needs of fellow-members of the community—knowing that the community provides a supportive network of mutual love. They love knowing that they will be loved in return. *'If there is this love among you, then everyone will know that you are my disciples'*, i.e. that you are learning from me (v.35). With an assurance of such supportive love, it may then be possible to venture on love to enemies that expect nothing in return (Luke 6:35).[3]

---

[3] Kenneth Grayston, *The Gospel of John: Epworth Commentaries* (London: Epworth Press, 1990), 113.

This common view further infers that the commandments given prior to Yeshua enshrine death and are earthly in nature. It implies that seeking to live in accordance with the Torah was in the absence of true love.[4] Harrison adds that John 13:34 "was new in that the love was to be exercised toward others not cause they belonged to the same nation, but because they belonged to Christ...[a]nd it was new because it was to be the expression of the peerless love of Christ, which the disciples had seen in life and would see also in death," yet later admits, "[t]hese commandments can be kept only in the power of the Holy Spirit"[5] (inferring that those prior to the ministry of Yeshua could not keep them). H. A. Ironside contends that John 13:34 should be thought of as the eleventh commandment, rounding off the Ten Commandments.[6]

The second possible interpretation is that it is simply a renewed commandment, one that enlarges what has been previously established, deepened by the teaching of the Messiah.[7] While commenting on 1 John 2:7, Joshua Brumbach adds, "[t]he commandment John mentions here is an 'old law' (i.e., 'from the beginning') because it is from the Torah (love your neighbor as yourself—Lev. 19:18), however, Yeshua's regular emphasis gave it further importance... a continuation and expansion of what was previously given."[8] This would be consis-

---

4   E. D. Burton, *The Epistle to the Galatians*, vol. 36, *International Critical Commentary* (London, U.K.: T&T Clark International, 1988), 274, 277, 280, 287, 291–92, 294.
5   Everett F. Harrison, "John," in *The Wycliffe Bible Commentary*, ed. Charles F. Pfeiffer & Everett F. Harrison (Chicago: Moody Publishers, 1990), 1103–1105.
6   H. A. Ironside, *John* (Grand Rapids: Kregel Publications, 2006), 324–331.
7   MacArthur, though not consistent in his application, admits it was "a new commandment ... in the sense that it presented a higher standard of love—one based on the example of the Lord Jesus Christ Himself." John MacArthur, *John: 12-21*, The MacArthur New Testament Commentary (Chicago, IL: Intervarsity Press, 2008), 89.
8   Joshua Brumbach, *John's Three Letters on Hope, Love and Covenant Fidelity: A Messianic*

tent with the methodology of Yeshua's teachings on the Sermon of the Mount (Matthew 5-7; "You have heard... But I say to you..."). As J. Carl Laney summarises:

> So what is "new" about the "new command"? It is the measure of the love "as I have loved you" and made Jesus' command "new" or "fresh" (*kainos*). John records that Jesus loved His own to the point of sacrificing His life (John 10:11; 15:12–13). Paul describes the same kind of sacrificial love in Ephesians 5:1–12. The measure of the disciple's love for others is determined by Christ's love for them.[9]

Hegg phrases it a slightly different way, stating that "we should understand that the 'old' can give birth to the 'new,' and in doing so, the 'old' does not cease to exist or become useless... to say it another way, 'old' can mean 'prior' and 'new' can mean 'current'... Thus, the old commandment which is summed in the very message of the Gospel, commanded to love God and to love one's neighbor."[10] Hence, the breadth and depth of the love of YHWH—what it means to love like him and whom to love—have been enlarged, not eradicated. It is correct to state that the love demonstrated by Yeshua was unlike anything before his incarnation. However, it should not to be seen as a change but rather a clarification of what had been corrupted after centuries of rabbinical influence in Israel. Hence, there is a "subtle

---

Commentary (Clarksville, MD: Lederer Books, 2019), 61-62.

9   J. Carl Laney, *John: Moody Gospel Commentary* (Chicago, IL: Moody Publishers,1992), 250; David Mishkin, *Rabbi & Redeemer: Discovering Yeshua in the Gospel of John* (Worthington, OH: Messianic Literature Outreach, 2010), 76.

10   Tim Hegg, *A Commentary on the Johannine Epistles: 1, 2, 3 John* (Tacoma, WA: TorahResource, 2018), 78.

but real rebuke to His disciples, for the love commandment had been constrained by the Jewish teachers to a parameter which God never intended."[11]

Of these two interpretations, only one maintains the continuity of the Torah's laws and does not see any portion of the Torah as being abolished. The first interpretation, widely accepted by Christians, is unfortunately shaped by a man-made theological framework that separates the body of believers and the laws of the Hebrew Scriptures from those in the Greek Scriptures. Exegetically, however, this approach is inconsistent with a "high bibliology" that upholds the unity and authority of all Scripture. As Scripture declares, the Torah is perfect (Psalms 19:7). Hence, John 13:34 must be a renewed commandment, which perfectly aligns with the understanding that Yeshua's covenant instituted at the last Passover before his death and resurrection was also an act of renewal (Luke 22:20).[12] The "exhortation to keep God's commandments is often part of the speeches before the making or renewing of the covenant in the OT tradition (Deut. 30:16; Exod 34:11; Josh 24:14–15)."[13] The standard of his expected love, as he loved us, is now broader and deeper in light of the incarnated Messiah's sacrificial work, but it does not replace or supersede the previous understanding of love established in the Hebrew Scriptures.

---

11 Ibid., 344.
12 Benjamin Szumskyj, "Chapters 3: Contending the Interpretation of a *Renewed* Covenant," in *The Laws of Torah in the Sanctification of the Modern Christian: A Brief Introduction to Pronomianism* (Wilmington, DE: Vernon Press, 2026).
13 Rekha Chennattu, *Johannine Discipleship as a Covenant Relationship* (Peabody, MA: Hendrickson Publishers, 2006), 85.

CHAPTER 2

AN EXEGESIS OF JOHN 14:15

What does Yeshua mean by the word "love" in John 14:15? The word "love" carries many different meanings across languages. Scripture itself speaks of several different types of love, each defined by the Greek word used and context of the passage. For example, there is the noun *storge* (στοργή), being familial love, "having the idea of family love or affection, as borne out by the negative adjective *astorgos* used only in Romans 1:31 and 2 Timothy 3:3."[1] There is also *eros* (ἔρως), "expressing a possessive love and used mainly of physical love...a love of the worthy and it is a love that desires to possess,"[2] and the verb *phileo* (φιλέω), one of the two commonly used words to denote "affectionate love characteristic of friendship...[its] derivatives *philo*, friend (used over twenty-nine times), and *philia*, (used only in James 4:4)... [denoting] a love that is warm and merited."[3] The final word is the noun *agape* (ἀγάπη), which has two forms: the adjective *agapētós* (ἀγαπητός), as seen in 1 John 2:7, and the verb *agapáō* (ἀγαπάω), as seen in John 14:15.

agapaō (ἀγαπάω)

According to William Mounce, before the Greek Scriptures, the verb *agapáō*:

---

1 D. H. Wheaton, "Love," in *Evangelical Dictionary of Theology*, ed. Walter A. Elwell (Grand Rapids, MI: Baker Academic, 2001), 709.
2 Ibid.
3 Ibid., 708.

An Exegesis of John 14:15

> ...was a colorless word without any great depth of meaning, used frequently as a synonym of *eros* (sexual love) and *phileo* (the general term for love). If it had any nuance it was the idea of love for the sake of its object. Perhaps because of its neutrality of meaning and perhaps because of this slight nuance meaning, the biblical writers picked *agapao* to describe many forms of human love... and most importantly, God's undeserved love for the unlovely. In other words, its meaning comes not from the Greek but from the biblical understanding of God's love. A biblical definition of love starts with God, never with us (1 Jn. 4:9–10).[4]

Scripturally, *agapáō* means "[t]o take a deep caring interest in someone or something... [and] denotes a deliberate choice, originating in the will and disposition of the agent and it is expressed by action."[5] In other words, it is an active love that does not seek to limit what is expected, but rather seeks to magnify a love, which becomes true only when placed into motion after being cognitively understood. Furthermore, "[t]he expression 'not to love' means to neglect, disregard, condemn (Rev. 12:11, meaning they condemned their lives even unto death, i.e. they willingly exposed themselves to death)."[6] Such love is resistant to action and limits expectations and the number of loving acts. *Agapáō* then, is not always used to denote the love of YHWH or the love his followers have towards one another. For example, Yeshua

---

[4] William D. Mounce, (ed.) "Love," in *Mounce's Complete Expositor Dictionary of Old & New Testament Words* (Grand Rapids, MI: Zondervan, 2006), 427.

[5] E. Richard Pigeon, *AMG's Comprehensive Dictionary of New Testament Words* (Chattanooga, TN: AMG Publishers, 2014), 640.

[6] Spiros Zodhiates, *The Complete Word Study Dictionary: New Testament* (Iowa Falls, IA: World Bible Publishers, 1992), 65.

comments that "the light has come into the world, and people loved [ἀγαπάω] darkness rather than light because their deeds were evil" (John 3:19). Later, he states that the Pharisees "loved [ἀγαπάω] human glory more than the glory that comes from God" (John 12:43). In 2 Timothy 4:10, the apostle Paul wrote that "Demas, in love [ἀγαπάω] with this present world, has deserted me and gone to Thessalonica." The use of love in all these instances denotes how the love intended for YHWH was willfully used to love what he hates. YHWH hates sin, not those commandments he expects believers to follow to avoid the practice of sin and the consequences of missing the mark.

Messiah Yeshua commands believers to "'Hear, O Israel! The Lord our God is one Lord; and you shall love [ἀγαπάω] the Lord your God with all your heart, and with all your soul, and with all your mind, and with all your strength… [and] You shall love [ἀγαπάω] your neighbor as yourself. There is no other commandment greater than these" (Mark 12:28-31). However, one has truly "heard" only when they have lived out that love practically. Hence, "[o]ur love toward Christ is demonstrated by our obedience to his teachings…[i]n return, this obedience invokes the blessing, of God's love for us (Jn. 14:21)."[7] G. Schneider puts it well:

> The world must recognize that Jesus has been sent by God and that God loves the disciples as he loved Jesus before the foundation of the world (17:23f., 26; cf. also 3:35; 10:17; 15:15f. regarding God's love for Jesus; 14:31 regarding Jesus' love for God). The love of Jesus for his own (11:5; 13:1, 34; 14:21; 15:9f., 12) was "love to the end"; it corresponds to the

---

7   William D. Mounce, (ed.) "Love," in *Mounce's Complete Expositor Dictionary of Old & New Testament Words* (Grand Rapids, MI: Zondervan, 2006), 427.

love of the Father and requires of the disciple that he keep the commandments of Jesus in order to remain in his love (15:9f). Thus the disciple, for his part, brings to realization his love for Jesus (14:15, 21, 23f., 28).[8]

Agapé conveys "His will to His children concerning their attitude toward one another [e.g. John 13:34] and toward all men," in that it "expresses the deep and constant love and interest of a perfect Being towards entirely unworthy objects, producing and fostering a reverential love in them towards the Giver *and a practical love towards those who are partakers of the same, and a desire to help others to seek the Giver.*"[9]

John teaches on this love not only through his writings but also by his actions as a pastor-teacher in the early church (see 3 John). As Andreas Köstenberger and David Crowther write, John's "ethic of leadership is one of love... [He] loves those entrusted to his spiritual care... [and the] extent of John's loving leadership is seen in 3 John, where the elder cannot bear to see Christian workers mistreated...provid[ing] a model of loving pastoral care and the self-denial necessary for any leader who has been called to serve the church."[10] All Christians are expected to receive YHWH's love and, in turn, love others as themselves (Matt. 22:37-40). However, doing so in leadership—loving those you lead with both intimacy and a sense of family, as John did—is striking.

---

8   G. Schneider, "ἀγάπη," in *Exegetical Dictionary of the New Testament*, Vol. 1, ed. Horst Balz and Gerhard Schneider (Grand Rapids, MI: William B. Eerdmans Publishing, 1990), 11.
9   W. E. Vine, "Agape" in *Vine's Expository Dictionary of Old & New Testament Words* (Nashville: Thomas Nelson Publishers, 1997), 693. Emphasis mine.
10 Andreas J. Köstenberger & David Crowther, "Leading with Love: Leadership in the Johannine Epistles" in *Biblical Leadership: Theology for the Everyday Leader*, ed. Benjamin K. Forrest, Chet Roden (Grand Rapids, MI: Kregel Publications, 2017), 482–483.

As such, this type of biblical love is essential for one called to lead the people of YHWH. Authentic love that looks beyond the proverbial idea that family is only by blood and goes directly to the spirit, reveals a leadership that focuses on the one thing that binds all believers in this life and the next: the saving grace of a loving deity that lovingly died as our substitutionary atonement. The Greek Scriptures are hallmarked by a love among believers and their leaders that is unmatched by any other civilization or nation, past or present. *Agapé* is countercultural and enshrines selflessness over selfishness. Today, the world defines love in ways that contradict what Scripture teaches and expects believers to practice toward one another. Granted, aspects of this love might be exampled by unbelievers, but truly biblical love is inconsistent with the world at large and is imperative in the leadership model for the local congregation. This love must be expressed and exampled by those who lead the contemporary church, to ensure a complete view of who God is and who his people are intended to be.

Love expressed by action is a testament to responding to the love enacted by Yeshua. He loved believers not only in creating them, rebirthing them by his Spirit, and in dying in their place, but by fulfilling the Torah as a model for them to follow *as an expression of love for him*. Morris stresses that this love—biblical love—is indeed active in its nature:

> God is concerned that men make the right response to his love, and he blesses those who do. Love leads to action; it is impossible to love someone deeply and not do things for him. Love is eager to serve, to give. So it is that the Old Testament writers link love with keeping God's commands. In fact, this is a relationship that God himself establishes: in the second commandment he speaks of "whose who love me and keep my

commandments" (Ex.20:6). Love and obedience go together... Thus the Old Testament in general and Deuteronomy in particular stress that God's people should not only receive his love but also actively return it.[11]

Many churchgoers today, understand that loving YHWH is evidenced through a series of goals and rituals, ranging from regular attendance, financial support, and fellowship, to being baptized, partaking in spiritual practices, and worship. There is nothing inherently wrong with any of these, especially when done so with conviction and intention, yet all share the same nature: *they are commandments* and all are *holy*. Each one is commanded of a believer, most of them originating prior to the Greek Scriptures. This is expected, as the means of sanctification for the ecclesia has remained unchanged since its inception at Mount Sinai. Through YHWH's progressive revelation, it was enlarged with the arrival of the Messiah and his teachings to both apostles and disciples. As mentioned above by Morris, to be exegetically consistent, a believer must understand that if the Torah is indeed a wedding contract, a gift from YHWH given in love. Receiving his love, in turn, means responding with love through action, namely by keeping his commandments. If this has indeed changed, then no amount of exegetical gymnastics can justify the idea that some of these commandments remain while the majority are no longer relevant, having been only for a historical ethnicity until the first century AD. Such antinomian teaching aligns more from the writings of Marcion of Sinope than with the pronomian teaching of Yeshua of Nazareth or writings of Paul of Tarsus.

---

11 Leon Morris, *Testaments of Love: A Study of Love in the Bible* (Grand Rapids: William B. Eerdmans, 1981), 42.

Furthermore, the often cited "Greatest Commandment" (Mark 12:28-31) is directly linked to the "Great Commission" (Matt. 28:16-20). At the end of his earthly ministry, Yeshua commands his disciples—and by extension, all disciples—*to teach all that he has commanded*.[12] Are we to understand that this pertains only to what he taught during the years with the twelve disciples or since the events of Mt. Sinai? The answer must be the latter, for after his ascension, the disciples gathered and observed Pentecost (Acts 2:1; 20:16; 1 Cor. 16:8), Sabbath (Acts 13:14, 42–44; 16:13), Unleavened Bread (Acts 20:6), and Yom Kippur (Acts 27:9). The disciples did not absolve themselves from any practice pertaining to the physical Temple before it fell (Acts 2:46, 21:26-30), nor the Torah as a whole (Acts 15:20–21). Hence, the commandments to be obeyed according to Yeshua were those that he had delivered at the birth of the ecclesia at Mt. Sinai (Exod. 12:38; Acts 7:38; cf. Ezek. 16:8). In leaving Egypt, the people were sanctified (Deut. 4:20; I Kings 8:51; Jer. 11:4). Yeshua's sermon on the hill in Northern Israel (Matthew 5–7) was meant to correct historical misinterpretations, not to abolish the Torah or establish a new set of commandments. He, like his breathed-out Word, remains the same yesterday, today, and forever (2 Tim. 3:16-17; Heb. 13:8).

tēreō (τηρέω)

To τηρέω ("keep") is to keep that which is important close enough, so as to guard it as precious (2 Tim. 4:7) or preserve it (Rev. 3:10). In John 14:15, the commandments of YHWH, the laws of Torah, are so precious to the believer that in observing them, their love for Yeshua is magnified. Keeping the commandments attests that their

---

12 For an excellent study of this passage, see Tim Hegg, *The Great Commission: How Yeshua Defines Taking God's Light into the World*, DVD (Tacoma, WA: TorahResource, 2016).

sanctification is a result of their saving faith, demonstrated through their works. The community of believers are not to be distinguished by comfort, but by conviction; it is a faith that is not cognitive but cultivating works that bear fruit. The "expressions used relative to Christians suggest the existence of a catechetical tradition…[and t]he disciples pass on this word of revelation with a summons to faith and obedience (Jn. 15:20) and keeping it means eternal life (8:51–52)."[13] As Johnson notes, "One's claim must be validated by one's conduct [and t]he evidence is obedience."[14] To "keep" is to know it in a way that conveys depth and understanding (e.g. Jer. 22:16, 31:33–34). To keep that which you own is to understand it, and depending on context, love it. Stern rightly notes the following:

> In the *Tanakh* the word "know" can mean "have intimate experience"; here "knowing Yeshua" means having intimate spiritual experience with him, to the degree that one obeys his commands from the heart. Anything less is not true knowledge; there is a difference between giving mental assent to Yeshua's Messiahship and know him. Elsewhere Yochanan [John] reports that Yeshua said, "If you love me, you will keep my commands," and "If you keep my commands you abide in my love [John 14;15, 15:10; cf. 14;21, 15;14]."[15]

---

13 H. Riesenfeld, "tēreō [to watch over, [protect]" in *Theological Dictionary of the New Testament: Abridged in One Volume* (Grand Rapids, MI: Wm. B. Eerdmans, 1985), 1175.
14 Thomas F. Johnson, *1, 2 & 3 John*, Understanding the Bible Commentary Series (Grand Rapids, MI: Baker Books, 1993), 40.
15 David H. Stern, *Jewish New Testament Commentary* (Clarksville, TN: Jewish New Testament Publications, 1992), 770.

The Gospel of John continues what he knew to be holy and true according to the Torah. In the book of Deuteronomy, YHWH interacts with unredeemed national Israel (which included redeemed Israel, i.e., the remnant) in a way that not only reveals himself as their sole Lord and Savior but also establishes how their relationship would operate through his revealed will, the Torah. His doctrines would shape the ecclesia in the wilderness. Deuteronomistic theology preserves the reality that obedience to YHWH in accordance with the Torah brings blessings, and that disobedience brings curses. What was true at the Christophany before Moses (Exod. 3:1–6; Acts 7:30–33) would be true when the incarnated Messiah's life was recorded by the disciple John. In the book of Deuteronomy, one of the most prominent themes is that of obedience. In Hebrew, obedience in a positive sense is expressed by *yiqqâhâh* (יִקְּהָה). However, when referring to false obedience, the word *kâchash* (כָּחַשׁ) is used, implying deception, insufficiency, and dishonesty—essentially, disobedience. While the term obedience does not appear liberally in Deuteronomy (as opposed to "obey," the Hebrew word שׁמע means "to hear" or "listen"), the concept and its application is evidenced as demonstrated in the wake of the many covenants and blessings to Israel instituted by YHWH. (It is often the obedience of the ecclesial remnant, cf. Isaiah 10:20-21, that ensures his blessings.) More significantly, obedience is strongly connected to love in the book of Deuteronomy. As Alexander notes, loving God "has very practical implications for the people…[as they] must fulfil the obligations placed on them in the covenant…[for] true love will demonstrate itself in perfect obedience."[16] He later notes that "Moses within his exhortations incorporates various comments to encourage obedience…[the]

---

16 T. Desmond Alexander, *From Paradise to the Promised Land: An Introduction to the Pentateuch* (Grand Rapids, MI: Baker Academic, 2012), 291.

most common motive is the promise of divine blessing" as exampled in the blessings promised in being generous to the poor as detailed in Deuteronomy 15:10.[17] Obedience, then, is strongly connected to the theology of blessings, as to be obedient to God results in blessings not expected or even deserved of, but given freely.[18]

In understanding the theme of obedience and the blessings that come from fulfilling this role, it is natural to also consider its opposite: disobedience and the connected theology of curses. Like obedience, the book of Deuteronomy strongly presents the theme of disobedience. While the Hebrew language does not have a specific word for disobedience, its concept and application are clearly taught, as seen in YHWH's judgments upon Israel. The majority of Israel's disobedience continued throughout the Hebrew Scriptures, as detailed in the writings of the major and minor prophets. Disobedience, then, is strongly connected to the theology of curses, as to be disobedient towards YHWH results in curses that are expected and even deserved, consistent with his unchanging holiness.

In Hebrew, the word "curse" is best understood through *'ârar* (אָרַר), a common term that does not appear in Deuteronomy, and *q^elâlâh* (קְלָלָה), which is also widely used and does appear in Deuteronomy. The latter word is meant to convey that YHWH allowed or directed punishment on an individual, group, or their property and resources. A

---

17 Ibid., 292.
18 Bârak (בָּרַךְ), which interestingly does not appear in Deuteronomy, means to "bless." Blessings then are supernatural promises manifested in the life of a believer in accordance with the will of YHWH and timing that is used to enhance their walk of faith, which in turn, results in the glorifying of YHWH and full obedience. This is evidenced through economic security (e.g. abundance of crops for harvest) to physical security (e.g. from warring neighbours). In the book of Deuteronomy, blessings (and curses) are explicitly documented in 28:1–68.

curse, then, in its Deuteronomic context, means wrongdoing befalling a specific person or people, as in Deuteronomy 28:16–68. It is more implied than explicitly stated. This is not the type of curse YHWH enacted on generations in the past (Exod. 20:5; 34:7; Num. 14:18; Deut. 5:9), the type YHWH hates and will punish eternally (Deut. 18:10–11; Rev. 21:8), or the type performed in accordance with a prophet's request (2 Kings 2:23–24). Rather, the curse spoken of here refers to judgment by YHWH in whatever form or manner he deems appropriate against those who disobey his will.

In the wake of the renewed covenant (Jer. 31:31–34) during Yeshua's last Passover meal (Luke 22:20; 1 Cor. 11:25), the blessings and curses of the Hebrew Scripture era are to be understood now in a Christological manner. There is no reason to consider that the way YHWH interacts with his ecclesia has changed. There is no Scripture suggesting that believers in the first century AD and thereafter understood obedience and blessings, disobedience and curses, differently from their spiritual ancestors. Believers are to be obedient, as Yeshua was obedient (cf. Phil. 2:8), and allegiance to him and his teachings reflect this obedience (cf. John 14:15). Disobedience, then, is to reject his lordship. Yeshua was a blessing and blessed others (cf. Rom. 15:29; 1 Cor. 10:16; Eph. 1:3). Also, in the Greek Scriptures, blessings are imparted from believers to one another (James 3:10; 1 Peter 3:9). While being a disobedient Christian does not mean one is no longer saved, it does prevent one from receiving blessings. (However, persistent disobedience may raise concerns about the authenticity of one's faith.) Consider the contrast between obedience and blessings versus disobedience and curses in the lives of Barnabas (Acts 4:36–37) and Ananias and Sapphira (Acts 5:1–11). Here, the former's obedience to YHWH and his people in selflessly giving his resources resulted in a blessed life and ministry, while the latter, whose disobedience to God and his people in selfishly keeping their resources, resulted in the curse of death itself. While the terms are not used, the theological concepts are evident. In the Greek Scriptures, one is "ready to punish all disobedience" (2 Cor. 10:6) and "receive[s] a just penalty" (Heb. 2:2). Additionally, Yeshua's salvific sacrifice was a blessing (cf. 1 Cor. 10:16; Gal. 4:15) and cannot be revoked, even in the wake of disobedience. The reality of salvation by a Christian will have them live an obedient walk of faith. So, despite the disobedience of those who believe in YHWH, he can still bless them. Salvation itself occurred when believers were "ungodly" (Rom. 5:6) and "dead in our transgressions" (Eph. 2:5). In this salvific context, then, disobedience will not result in curses from YHWH (as curses are understood through Scripture), but it will affect the Christian's spiritual growth and development and possible denial of their petitioned prayers.

entolē (ἐντολή)

In John 8:51–52, Yeshua declares that those who τηρήσῃ ("keep") his λόγον ("word") "will never see death." This word refers to the Torah, which at that time comprised "all Scripture" (2 Tim. 3:16-17), meaning the Hebrew Scriptures. Over time, this understanding enlarged to include the Greek Scriptures, as seen in 1 Timothy 5:18 (cf. Deut. 25:4; Luke 10:7).[19] To contend that the laws of Yeshua in the first century AD differ from, supersede, or cancel those he gave to the prophet Moses (with God the Father and God the Holy Spirit) creates an unnecessary division. This perspective only strengthens the

---

19   Stephen D. Renn, ed., "Commandment," in *Expository Dictionary of Bible Words* (Peabody, MA: Hendrickson Publishers, 2005), 199; Spiros Zodhiates, "ἐντολή *entolē*," in *The Complete Word Study Dictionary: New Testament* (Iowa Falls, IA: World Bible Publishers, 1992), 594.

tradition of the tripart nature of the Torah or belief that the so-called "New" Covenant replaced the "Old" Covenant.[20] However, a handful of scholars disagree.[21] The "Great Commission" further affirms that all that has been taught by Messiah Yeshua, from Mt. Sinai to the Sermon on the Mount and through his disciples, are to be observed (Matt. 28:16–20). This includes observance of the appointed festivals, kashrut, and other commandments that are expected of those being grafted into a pre-existing covenantal community, one that has existed for thousands of years prior to the arrival of the Messiah.

Entolē (ἐντολή) refers to commandments, which Yeshua contends encompass the entire Hebrew Scriptures, according to Matthew 22:36–40. While speaking of the command to love (John 13:34), Yeshua does not nullify the laws of the Torah but rather summarises them, reminding his audience that, at its core, the law is love. The commandments were not to be understood as authoritarian, as some have sought to frame them.[22] They were created by God, who is love (1 John 4:8; ἀγάπη), and are to be responded to with obedient love (John 14:15, 21, 23; ἀγαπάω). G. Schrenk remarks on how the commandment of love protects believers from spiritual harm:

---

20 For a rebuttal against these theological claims, see: Benjamin Szumskyj, "Chapters 2–3," in *The Laws of Torah in the Sanctification of the Modern Christian: A Brief Introduction to Pronomianism* (Wilmington, DE: Vernon Press, 2026).

21 M. Limbeck, "ἐντολή," in *Exegetical Dictionary of the New Testament*, Vol. 1, ed. Horst Balz and Gerhard Schneider (Grand Rapids, MI: William B. Eerdmans Publishing, 1990), 461. He contends that the use of ἐντολή in the Johannie literature has nothing to do with laws of the Torah, but somehow, does in all other references in the Greek Scriptures.

22 "*Commands* are military orders, and obedience (i.e. 'do what you are told') is the ominous virtue of a police state… [o]beying commands may be important in emergencies, but it cannot be the standard requirement of a Christian community." Kenneth Grayston, *The Gospel of John*, Epworth Commentaries (London, UK: Epworth Press, 1990), 119.

In the Johannine Epistles the following features are to be noted. [A)] The *entolaí* are always related to the one *entolḗ* of love. [B)] The sharper conflict with Gnosticism leads to a heavier stress on keeping God's commandments (1 Jn. 2:3; 3:22; 5:3; 2 Jn. 4). True understanding of love for God must be opposed to mystical union, and love of God must be strictly related to love of the brethren. [C)] The description of the *entolḗ* as both old and new is directed against the Gnostic love of novelty. [D)] Also aimed at Gnosticism is the relating of faith and the *entolḗ* (1 Jn. 3:23) and the insistence that the commandments are not grievous (5:3). The law does not pose a problem, as in Paul, for the *entolḗ* is bound up with faith and the battle is against antinomian Gnosticism. There is no true gnosis without *entolḗ* (1 Jn. 2:3-4), but there are no *entolaí* without the *entolḗ* linked to Jesus, and as in the Gospel, though less explicitly, keeping the commandments is keeping the word. Revelation, too, links God's commands to Jesus and witness to him (cf. 12:17; 14:12). 2 Peter is directed against libertinism and understandably calls Christian teaching *entolḗ* in 2:21 and 3:2. The *entolḗ* of 1 Tim. 6:14, however, is the charge that is committed to Timothy.[23]

It would be both inconsistent and problematic to contend that the historical allegiance to the Torah—an expression of love through obedience and evidenced by Yeshua in his spiritual battles (Matt.

---

[23] G. Schrenk, "Commandment," in *Theological Dictionary of the New Testament: Abridged in One Volume*, ed. Geoffrey W. Bromiley (Grand Rapids, MI: Wm. B. Eerdmans, 1985), 237.

4:1–11)—should now to be abandoned and replaced with a new body of laws, most of which mirror the very ones that were supposedly discarded. In the Hebrew Scriptures, heretical theology existed as well, from false prophets (Deut. 13:1–5) and syncretism (1 Kings 12:28) to iconolatry (Judges 17:3-5, 8:24–27). Thus, the *entolē* (ἐντολή) that defended against and destroyed the false ideologies and theologies of the Greek Scripture era are the same as those that were used against the false teachers and teachings of the Hebrew Scripture era. Much of mainstream Christianity's descent into false teaching, heresy, and worldly accommodation, is its instance on embracing commandments and ideologies outside of the ecclesia because it cultivates antagonism towards that which YHWH has already established: his Torah. Generation after generation has annulled the Scriptures (cf. John 10:35), dividing them into two canons, and abrogating two-thirds of its commandments in favour of comfort, experientialism, and tradition. Scripture promises, though, that the Holy Spirit would help us to keep them (Ezek. 36:27). Furthermore, Hegg is incredibly helpful in highlighting that ἐντολή "refers to Yeshua's commandment to love one another and not to the commandments of God as a whole cannot be sustained by its use in the Tanach," citing the singular use of the Hebrew word מִצְוָה (mitzvah, "commandment") in Deuteronomy 6:1, 7:11, 17:20, 2 Kings 17:37, and 2 Chronicles 14:4.[24] Again, the unity of Scripture affirms a correct understanding of the term.

Excursus: On Discipleship

The best definition of a disciple comes from Matthew 10, in which Yeshua calls and sends out the twelve disciples. It is here we

---

24 Tim Hegg, *A Commentary on the Johannine Epistles: 1, 2, 3 John* (Tacoma, WA: TorahResource, 2018), 67–68.

An Exegesis of John 14:15

learn a great deal, ranging from the ability to perform supernatural acts (Matt. 10:8), to total dependence upon YHWH for all things (Matt. 10:9–11), to the anticipated persecution that comes with being a Christian (Matt. 10:17–23), all the way to pronouncing the truth of YHWH (Matt. 10:26–27), prioritizing him in your personal life (Matt. 10:35–37) and the rewards of servitude (Matt. 10:40-42). These truths would have been reinforced to Matthias upon replacing Judas as one of the disciples (Acts 1:20-26). As disciples, we must place Yeshua first and foremost (Mark 8:34-38) and follow his teachings (John 15:5-8) without excuse or compromise. *We are all disciples.*

Disciples emulate the Master and abide in all his ways. As such, working from Matthew 10, a disciple *perseveres* in the ways of YHWH, *pronounces* only his truth, and *prioritises* his existence before their own (cf. John 14:6). They have been saved from sin and into holiness. Their salvation has been eternally sealed by the Holy Spirit, who empowers them with fruit and gifts, while sanctifying them as they are conformed into the image of Messiah Yeshua. There is no other way to life, no other path considered by them, for YHWH will ensure that from justification, through sanctification and culminating in glorification, the perseverance of the saint. From the Scriptures, a follower of Yeshua is someone who *pronounces* only the truth of YHWH. They preach the whole counsel of YHWH through action, deeds and words. They live in accordance with the revealed truths of Scripture and abide in him, for by practising his commandments they love him, and by fulfilling them they preserve the presence of righteousness. They live by the moral absolutes of YHWH, and both share and teach them regardless of culture and season. Their identity is in Yeshua. Without him, they are nothing, and with him they have everything. They desire more of him and less of themselves. They are wholly dependent on YHWH and know that their lives belong to him, for he created them and will usher them into the afterlife. If they live, they live for the Lord, or if they die, they die for the Lord; therefore, whether they live or die, they are his. YHWH is their first and foremost love. Furthermore, discipleship must be centred on the Tri-Unity, community, and Scriptures.

Discipleship is centred on the Tri-Unity. The process of developing followers of Yeshua involves believing in God the Father, God the Son, and God the Holy Spirit. Discipleship is the spiritual bridge between the believer upon salvation and their arrival into the New Heavens and Earth. It is interwoven into their sanctification, essential to their spiritual maturity, and the means of being conformed into the image of Yeshua (Rom. 8:29). Discipleship, understood and embarked on biblically, ensures a healthy community of believers, one which has a high view of doctrine and values the relational manner by which those made alive in Messiah Yeshua are led by the Holy Spirit in order to glorify God the Father.

Discipleship is centred on Community. The process of developing followers of Yeshua involves all aspects that make up "the Body of Christ" to function in unison, working both individually and collectively (cf. 1 Cor. 12:15–20), with interdependence rather than independence. Unity, then, is essential, as each member is interdependent and is sustained from the same source, being God the Father, God the Son, and God the Holy Spirit. This will be achieved because of disciples who are committed to integrating biblical truths from the Scriptures into their lives and practices them within themselves and in harmony with their saved brethren. Communities constantly need to strive for the spiritual health of its members, each being unique as the other and knowing that regardless of so-called position and power, we are equal in dependence on Yeshua.

Discipleship is centred on the Scriptures. The process of developing followers of Yeshua involves both discernment (from falsehoods and impurities), nourishment (spiritual in this context), and (scriptural) teaching, reproof, correction, and training (in righteousness; cf. 2 Tim. 3:16–17). Essentially, discipleship is goal orientated towards health (mental, physical, and spiritual) because all members of the church are being conformed into the image of the Son (Rom. 8:29), the embodiment of perfection and the one whom disciples all believers.

In conclusion, disciples both create, and are created by, disciples. After his resurrection and before his ascension, Messiah Yeshua pronounced several great commissions. These then will form the basis to help people connect to Christ, connect to one another, and connect to the mission of YHWH. In Matthew 28:16–20, he commands Christians to baptize unbelievers in the name of the Father, and of the Son, and of the Holy Spirit. As such, we must teach and preach the God of Israel, raise up disciples within all cultures and generations, and undergo a ritual that does not save, but shows obedience to YHWH and ushers their arrival into his family. In Mark 16:14–18, he declares that disciples will be able to perform signs as they mission, while unbelievers who reject the good news will be condemned. As such, we are to utilize our spiritual gifts and preach, teach, and disciple, and warn about the reality of living outside the presence of YHWH, his will, and his salvation (and the reality of Hell). Luke 24:44–49 stresses Yeshua's fulfilment of promises in the Hebrew Scriptures and the importance of understanding what was achieved through his crucifixion. As such, we must teach and preach the entire Word of God, both the Hebrew and Greek Scriptures, and continually focus on the importance of what Yeshua achieved on the cross. Finally, John 20:19–23 emphasizes the peace of a relationship with YHWH and the forgiveness of sins as paramount when sharing the good news. As such, Christians must be discipled in both the war of the world and the peace of YHWH, in addition to the reality and nature of sin—something that must be acknowledged and dealt with on a daily basis.

CHAPTER 3

PARALLEL PASSAGES IN JOHANNINE LITERATURE

There are several passages in Johannine literature that repeat or echo the statement made by Yeshua in John 14:15. It is necessary to explore these passages to see whether they, too, affirm the view that the apostle John was indeed referring to the totality of Torah.

In the remainder of the Gospel of John, we see the disciple make similar statements that are intended to both affirm and reinforce the importance of what Yeshua was teaching (John 14:21, 23).[1] As Chennattu remarks, "Like the OT covenant relationship, Jesus describes discipleship in terms of relationship characterized by mutual love, fidelity, and obedience to the covenant commandments (vv. 15, 21, 23–24)."[2] John feels no need to divide the Torah into sections, nor is he concerned that the audience, past or present, would misunderstand what is meant by the "commandments." Redeemed Gentiles would have not considered that some commandments were intended to be ongoing while others were abrogated. Instead, further reading of the Greek Scriptures reveals that love does not abolish commandments but rather serves as their source and intended goal in practising faithful works.

---

1 MacArthur notes, "This is the third time in the section (vv. [14:]15,21) that Christ linked obedience with genuine love for Him (cf. 8:31)." John MacArthur, *John: 12–21*, The MacArthur New Testament Commentary (Chicago, IL: Intervarsity Press, 2008), 118.
2 Rekha Chennattu, *Johannine Discipleship as a Covenant Relationship* (Peabody, MA: Hendrickson Publishers, 2006), 111.

John 15:10 states, "If you keep My commandments, you will abide in My love; just as I have kept My Father's commandments and abide in His love." This simply refers to the disposition of obedience, meaning that Yeshua abided in the commandments exclusively given to him by God the Father in relation to his earthly ministry (cf. John 10:18, 12:49–50, 14:31). Likewise, all disciples are to have the same heart when it comes to all that Yeshua has commanded. The commandments between God the Father and his Son are naturally different from those given to his creation, but what is identical, is the disposition of the one receiving the instructions from the divine.

1 John 2:3 refers to commandments and is not in the singular. D. Edmond Hiebert stresses that the "conditional formulation challenges each one to examine himself to discover whether he fulfills the condition… [for t]he one who has been brought into a saving relationship with God finds within himself a growing love for and desire to obey his commands… [s]uch a keeping of God's command is not legalism but a voluntary internalization of His commands as a pattern for practical conduct."[3] It is an indefatigable obedience. Brumbach adds that "John wants his audience to have a similar kind of faith [to his own], one that is solid, rooted in Torah, and the history and experience of Israel, as understood through Yeshua's life and teachings, and as reliably passed on by the original apostles."[4] Gary Derickson affirms that the commandments referenced here pertain to the Hebrew Scriptures rather than the Greek Scriptures, which had not yet been canonized in the first century AD. He notes that the term "commandments"

---

[3] D. Edmond Hiebert, *The Epistles of John: An Expositional Commentary* (Greenville, SC: Bob Jones University Press, 1991), 79–80.

[4] Joshua Brumbach, *John's Three Letters on Hope, Love and Covenant Fidelity: A Messianic Commentary* (Clarksville, MD: Lederer Books, 2019), 60.

is "a common term in the LXX, occurring more than two hundred times, most often translating the Hebrew מִצְוָה ("commandment")... [and i]ts use indicates the general body of precepts most often rather than specific command, whether singular or plural."[5] This is consistent with Yeshua's instance that he has not come to abolish any part of the Torah.[6] Thomas Johnson, however, insists the context indicates that the commandments referred to here pertain to loving YHWH and others, citing the absence of other "moral or ethical" concerns throughout the epistle.[7] This is odd, as it fails to consider that in order to love, one must be taught how to love, which is the very blueprint of the Torah.

In 1 John 5:3, John remarks that Yeshua's commandments are not burdensome. The Messiah employed the same language in his earthly ministry (Matt. 11:28–30) and as one member of the Tri-Unity (Deut. 30:11–14). The yoke of the Torah is not a burden, but the yoke of ungodly marriage of written and oral laws are (Mark 7:8; Acts 15:10; cf. b. *Shabbat* 31a; b. *Yevamot* 47a–b). As Hegg notes, "in adding their own commandments and teaching that they had divine authority equal to or even greater than the Torah of Moses, they put a burden upon the people that was difficult, if not impossible to bear,"[8] as attested in Matthew 23:4. At this point, it is crucial to emphasize that pronomianism rejects legalism while ensuring that rightful criticism of man-made laws does not lead to the dismissal of YHWH's commandments. This

---

5   Gary W. Derickson, *1, 2 & 3 John: Evangelical Exegetical Commentary* (Bellingham, WA: Lexham Press, 2014), 135–136.

6   Tim Hegg, *A Commentary on the Johannine Epistles: 1, 2, 3 John* (Tacoma, WA: TorahResource, 2018), 67.

7   Thomas F. Johnson, *1, 2 & 3 John*, Understanding the Bible Commentary Series (Grand Rapids: Baker Books, 1993), 40.

8   Tim Hegg, *A Commentary on the Johannine Epistles: 1, 2, 3 John* (Tacoma, WA: TorahResource, 2018), 269.

is far more common than one realises, and many commentators fail to distinguish these laws when condemning the laws referred to in Scripture. Simply defined, legalism "mean[s] simply adding human rules to the law of God and teaching these human rules as the way of Christian obedience."[9] It undermines the will of God the Father, seeks to contribute to the finished work of God the Son, and willingly grieves God the Holy Spirit. This is abhorrent and should be loudly rebuked and disciplined in the local congregation. Jerram Barrs notes that legalism is front and center during the ministry of Yeshua and his attacks against the scribes and Pharisees, whose righteousness was corrupted by hypocrisy, human rules, and by replacing the commandments of YHWH with their own, thereby nullifying the commandments of YHWH.[10] As such, it is disappointing to read that Thomas Johnson slips into the tired old contention that the Torah and its commandments are burdensome, whereas those of Yeshua are light,[11] seemingly forgetting that Yeshua authored the Torah and did not abolish it. The additions of man, the teachings of the elders, are what were burdensome. Uncomfortably, if everyone who practises sin also practises lawlessness (1 John 3:4), wouldn't removing the majority of commandments from the Torah be the very definition of antinomianism?[12] Oddly, in commenting on 2 John 1:6, Johnson further remarks that "love is defined by walking according to his command...[and] the heart of all God's commands

---

9   Jerram Barrs, *Delighting in the Law of the Lord: God's Alternative to Legalism and Moralism* (Wheaton, IL: Crossway, 2013), 179.
10 Ibid., 192–198.
11 Thomas F. Johnson, *1, 2 & 3 John*, Understanding the Bible Commentary Series (Grand Rapids, MI: Baker Books, 1993), 121.
12 Tim Hegg, *A Commentary on the Johannine Epistles: 1, 2, 3 John* (Tacoma, WA: TorahResource, 2018), 270.

is love (v. 6b; Matt. 22:37–40; Rom. 13:8; Gal. 5:14; 1 Tim 1:5)."[13] William Loader makes the following observation regarding the verse:

> [It] holds in tension obligation and spontaneous natural response. Love is a command. Conscious choice is involved. Yet we are not dealing with a command or a set of commands which are *burdensome*. They do not sit unnaturally on our shoulders as an awkward and heavy weight. The reason they are not burdensome is not primarily that they make few demands; on the contrary, the call to love is a call to be self-giving which can be costly. Rather, they are not *burdensome*, because, as the author has just pointed out, they follow naturally from who we are as children of God. We are in relationship with the one who loves us and whose love enables us, in turn, to love and so fulfill his commands.[14]

What Yeshua commanded during his earthly ministry does not conflict with what he taught at Mt. Sinai as a member of the Tri-Unity. John is not saying in this verse that Yeshua's commandments are easier or less burdensome than those he previously gave. He is not saying that the Torah is a burden or that, having failed previously, Yeshua has now introduced a new body of commandments that will be less burdensome. Such an idea would be preposterous. John echoes the language of Deuteronomy 30:11–14 and reminds his readers that Yeshua has

---

13   Thomas F. Johnson, *1, 2 & 3 John*, Understanding the Bible Commentary Series (Grand Rapids, MI: Baker Books, 1993), 154.
14   William Loader, *The Johannine Epistles: Epworth Commentaries* (London, UK: Epworth Press, 1992), 61. Earlier on p.17, in commenting on 1 John 5:3, the author remarks "[t]he evidence of knowing God is not verbal claims but a particular life-style characterized by keeping God's commands."

always intended his holy instructions to be a blessing. As Gary Derickson writes, "John has all of God's will in view, not just the command to love one another... 'For why are the commands not burdensome? God enables us to keep them.'"[15]

Finally, in 2 John 1:6, we are reminded that love is covenantal language and that "we are to follow God, adhere to his mitzvot, and live in covenantal obedience."[16] It is magnified in community with those who also obey and serve YHWH. The foundational work that is Torah ensures that believers are prepared to discern the false teachers and their works (2 John 1:7–11). In this passage, while the verse before it is in the singular (i.e., "commandment"), verse 6 speaks in the plural (*tas entolas*), which makes sense considering that John is making a connection that the ultimate command to love YHWH is evidenced by obeying his commandments.[17] Love fulfills the Torah (Rom. 13:8–10; Gal. 5:14). Again, one *walks* the way according to the Torah (Deut. 30:16; 2 John 1:6). Yeshua "is not diminishing the Torah, but describing the high watermark of true obedience...[and] the freedom we have in Messiah is freedom from the curse of the Torah"[18] and filled by the Holy Spirit, we can now live it out. Derickson insists that the phrase "you have heard from *the beginning*, his command is that you walk in love" in 2 John 1:6 (italics mine) pertains exclusively to John's audi-

---

15 Gary W. Derickson, *1, 2 & 3 John: Evangelical Exegetical Commentary* (Bellingham, WA: Lexham Press, 2014), 498–499.
16 Joshua Brumbach, *John's Three Letters on Hope, Love and Covenant Fidelity: A Messianic Commentary* (Clarksville, MD: Lederer Books, 2019), 129–130.
17 D. Edmond Hiebert, *The Epistles of John: An Expositional Commentary* (Greenville, SC: Bob Jones University Press, 1991), 300.
18 Tim Hegg, *A Commentary on the Johannine Epistles: 1, 2, 3 John* (Tacoma, WA: TorahResource, 2018), 348.

ence.¹⁹ However, one cannot help but wonder why this phrase could not also align with 1 John 2:7, where "the beginning" refers to that which was taught in the Mosaic Covenant.²⁰ While differing on the timing, I agree with Georg Strecker that the phrase refers back to the birth of the ecclesia:

> Central to [John's] writing is not a new commandment but the one "we have had from the beginning" (v.5), "just as you have heard it from the beginning" (v.6). The ἀρχῇ to which he refers is not thought of in an absolute sense, as the beginning of the world's creation, but describes the beginning of the church, the founding of the Christian community. The construction with the first or second person plural excludes nan identification with Christ's preaching, although the Christ-event represents the foundation of the community's faith. But even in this case it is clear that the idea of tradition implies the notion of a past time to which [John] the presbyter can refer in order to give binding instructions for the present.²¹

As we have seen, these parallel passages in Johannine literature support a pronomian interpretation of John 14:15, which sees the "commandments" as including the Law of Moses. John's consistent call

---

19 Gary W. Derickson, *1, 2 & 3 John: Evangelical Exegetical Commentary* (Bellingham, WA: Lexham Press, 2014), 613–614.

20 Again, "The commandment John mentions here is an 'old law' (i.e., "from the beginning") because it is from the Torah (love your neighbor as yourself – Lev. 19:18)." Joshua Brumbach, *John's Three Letters on Hope, Love and Covenant Fidelity: A Messianic Commentary* (Clarksville, MD: Lederer Books, 2019), 61.

21 Georg Strecker, *The Johannine Letters*, trans. Linda M. Maloney, ed. Haold W. Attridge (Minneapolis, MN: Fortress Press, 1996), 232.

to obey the commandments is a call to obey the commandments found in the Hebrew Scriptures, not just those given in the Greek Scriptures. Rather than nullifying the Torah, these passages emphasize that love and obedience to YHWH's commandments remain fundamental to the believer's life.

Excursus: WWJD? His Commandments!

Messiah Yeshua's life and character were meant to serve as our example (cf. 1 Pet. 2:21; John 13:15). Empowered by his Holy Spirit, we are being conformed into his image (Rom. 8:29), for whoever "keeps His word, in him the love of God has truly been perfected... [for b]y this we know that we are in Him: the one who says he abides in Him ought himself to walk in the same manner as He walked" (1 John 2:5–6). Though we will *not become* Yeshua, we are to be *like* him, emulating his actions, thoughts, and words (cf. John 13:15); we are to be godly, not divine. In his first coming, Yeshua declared a clear mission (Luke 4:17–21). As our example, believers are to follow in his footsteps and live according to the Great Commandment (Matt. 22:37–40) and carry out the Great Commission he started (Matt. 28:16–20).

In His Steps by Charles Sheldon follows minister Henry Maxwell, who teaches his congregation to be more like Yeshua after his own sinful actions expediated the death of a homeless man. The novel emphasizses what a believer must *do* more than what a believer must *know*. In its sequel, *Jesus is Here!* (1914), Sheldon appealed to the believing generation after World War I, recognizing that while they knew right from wrong, this awareness had not prevented the events that resulted in World War I and the loss of life it resulted in. A devotional classic, the book focused on what it truly means to be like the Messiah[22] and to imitate God (*imitatio dei*), which Sheldon believed involved addressing the plights of modern society. Sheldon was a Christian socialist and believed in a social gospel, one that overemphasised the actions of Christians in addressing social issues and underemphasizing doctrinal knowledge and teaching. Head knowledge, as described in *In His Steps*, would not bring people to salvation, but compassionate actions would.

Sheldon's understating of God and the Scriptures persists today, finding sanctuary in the social gospel that dominates much of the twenty-first century. His evangelical ethics have been mirrored by those pioneering this movement, saying, "The evangelical church does not need another war over the Bible…[w]e need people who are captivated by the moral vision of the kingdom of God."[23] This is a reversal of the Great Commandment (Matt. 22:37–40) in terms of hierarchal importance. The "What Would Jesus Do" movement (WWJD) that began with the release of the book, while unique, pronounced an incomplete Yeshua. While believers should understand and follow what Yeshua did (e.g., keeping his commandments), they must also grasp why he did it, for whom he did it, where he instructed it to be done, and when he declared it permissible. As Juan Sánchez rightly notes, "Christians too often apply this 'imitation of Christ' only to ethical situations… The unintended result is that Jesus gets reduced to a teacher of morals." Sánchez continues, "it is true that we are called to imitate Christ… [b]ut too often, we don't think carefully about what this imitation looks like and what it will cost us…Imitation of Christ requires meditation

---

22 Klaus Issler, "Jesus' Example: Prototype of the Dependent, Spirit-Filled Life," in *Jesus in Trinitarian Perspective: An Intermediate Christology*, ed. Fred Sanders and Klause Issler (Nashville, TN: B&H Publishing Group, 2007) 194.

23 Wyndy Corbin Reuschling, *Reviving Evangelical Ethics: The Promises and Pitfalls of Classic Models of Morality* (Grand Rapids, MI: Brazos Press, 2008), 113.

on Christ."[24] The "steps" Sheldon wrote about, were of a Yeshua more human than wholly human *and* divine, *more pragmatic* than doctrinal. The "good" that Sheldon sought, while well intentioned, pronounced a gospel focused on humanity rather than the one focused on who made humanity, the Tri-Unity. Sheldon's Messiah-like activity sounds biblical, but action and the resultant unity in the absence of doctrine is not fruit consistent with the Scriptures. Faith without works is the same as works without faith (James 2:14–26).

Sheldon's *In His Steps*, while interesting, is not a helpful introduction to the Messiah of Scripture. His socialist leanings and embrace of the social gospel suggests that his pastoral desire for believers is not historically orthodox and could be interpreted as aligning more with the world than the Word. While a novel approach to the debate of Christian belief and practise, in talking the talk and walking the walk, its strength lies more in learning what not to do when seeking to live out the example of Yeshua the Messiah.

---

[24] Juan Sánchez, "What Did Jesus Do?" *The Gospel Coalition* (October 2012). https://www.thegospelcoalition.org/article/what-did-jesus-do/.

CHAPTER 4
A PRONOMIAN INTERPRETATION OF JOHN 14:15

Now that we have examined the various interpretations of this verse and the definitions of the Greek words used, we can develop a more probable interpretation of John 14:15. The verse is a conditional sentence: "If you love Me" (*protasis*), then "you will keep My commandments" (*apodasis*). More specifically, it is a third-class conditional sentence, also known as a more probable future condition, where the *protasis* is formed using ἐάν along with a verb in the subjunctive mood in any tense. In this instance, however, it must be in the present tense, because it is a general conditional with reference to the present (i.e., if you obey YHWH by loving him now, then you will obey YHWH by living his commandments continually). As Laney states, the "present tense is used in both verbs and could be rendered, 'If you keep on loving… you will keep on obeying,' [for o]ne's love for Christ is measured by obedience [and c]ontinued love for Christ serves as a preventative against disobedience." He adds, "the genuineness of our love is most effectively communicated through actions."[1] While the first part of John 14:15 is recognized as being in the present tense with an imperfective aspect, the second part is more likely a simple "future indicative verb as found here (*tērēsete* [τηρήσετε]), "you will keep") [because it] is a way of expressing an imperative thought that also contains a hint of promise… [and t]he ancient Greek version of the Ten Commandments uses the same syntax, a future indicative where one might expect

---

1   J. Carl Laney, *John: Moody Gospel Commentary* (Chicago, IL: Moody Publishers,1992), 260–261.

the imperative mood."[2] Hence, this was not a love bound to a body of holy instructions that would cease within years of the statement being made because of Yeshua's death and resurrection; it was an obedient love that would continue throughout the life of the disciples, before and after the cross, and to be emulated by all redeemed generations of those who would seek to follow the way of the Messiah. That this verse is repeated in 1 John 5:3 confirms this reality. Keeping the laws of the Torah is therefore dependent on loving God (cf. Mark 12:28–31). Since Yeshua is one with YHWH, fully divine and human, loving him is also a commandment. To love him is to demonstrate obedience in accordance with his Torah, which commands believers to love him. To suggest that some commandments are no longer operative, would be to contend that the spoken words of YHWH are now redundant written words. Plainly stated, works demonstrate faith in loving YHWH. It is a humble disposition and one that cultivates uncompromising obedience.[3] A believer does not first keep the commandments in order to affirm their love for YHWH any more than a believer can attest of their love of YHWH yet fail to keep his commandments.

---

2   Karen H. Jobes, *John: Through Old Testament Eyes* (Grand Rapids: Kregel Academic, 2021), 229. Consider also that in John 14:24 that there is no differentiate between the word (teaching) and words of Yeshua in the use of λόγος (logos) and the words of YHWH (Deuteronomy 5:5).

3   "The person who is truly humble before God is also humble before God's Word. God says He esteems the person who is humble and contrite in spirit and trembles at His Word... Josiah realized that the Word of God was the expression of the will of God, that it was to be obeyed, and that failure to obey would incur the judgement of God. Because Josiah trembled ay the Word of God, his heart was responsive, he humbled himself, he acknowledged the sin of his people. And God heard him. He did not dispute the Word of God; he simply obeyed it." Jerry Bridges, *The Fruitful Life* (Colorado Springs, CO: NavPress, 2006), 50.

Keener makes the following astute observation:

> The section heavily emphasizes love for Jesus and the association of love for him with keeping his commandments. Keeping the commandments (in the context, especially love—13:34–35) seems a prerequisite for acquiring or continuing in the activity of the Spirit. God's blessings also were often conditional on keeping his commandments, as in 14:15 (e.g., Exod 15:26). Early Judaism generally believed in the renewal rather than the abrogation of Torah in the end time [*Abot R. Nat.* 4A; b. *Ta'an.* 19b, *bar.*; *Pesiq. Rab.* 52:3]. Faith and love, the central requirements of the covenant in Deuteronomy, also appear as the basic requirements here; in biblical covenant tradition, those who love God will keep his commandments (Exod 20:6; Deut 5:10; 7:9; 11:1, 13; 30:16). Thus, for John as for the law, love is not mere sentiment but defined by specific content through God's commandments.[4]

This direct connection back to the time of Moses when the Torah was given by YHWH raises the question of why such an antinomian spirit continues throughout Church history. If one's definition of fulfillment results in the Torah being abolished, then it cannot be considered anything other than an affront to YHWH and his Word.[5] Yeshua's ref-

---

4 Craig S. Keener, *The Gospel of John: 2 Volumes* (Grand Rapids, MI: Baker Academic, 2010), 934.

5 Benjamin Szumskyj, "Chapter 2: Defining, Redefining, and Defending Pronomianism and its Tenets," in *The Laws of Torah in the Sanctification of the Modern Christian: A Brief Introduction to Pronomianism* (Wilmington, DE: Vernon Press, 2026); David Wilber, *How Jesus Fulfilled the Law: A Pronomian Pocket Guide to Matthew 5:17–20* (Clover, SC: Pronomian Publishing, 2011).

erence to the commandments affirms continuity, not discontinuity, for the same spiritual disposition towards the Torah upheld by the spiritual descendants of the first-century believers is to be maintained towards both the Hebrew Scriptures and the Greek Scriptures.

The commandments of YHWH are not tripartite in nature but are both moral and universal, distinguishable only in their designation by gender and lineage. To contend and insist, according to human tradition, that the laws of Torah are to be understood as ceremonial, civil, and moral, and that the first two of these have been abrogated, is an affront to the holiness of YHWH and the ongoing nature of his Word. Tim Hegg perceptively notes the following:

> If we read the Torah with the purpose of discovering whether categories of ceremonial, civil, and moral laws are clearly delineated, we discover that just the opposite is true. Commandments governing all aspects of life are woven together in a unified manner. We may take Exodus 22:19–29 as an example[:] **Moral:** 19 "Whoever lies with an animal shall surely be put to death. 20 "He who sacrifices to any god, other than to the LORD alone, shall be utterly destroyed. **Civil:** 21 "You shall not wrong a stranger or oppress him, for you were strangers in the land of Egypt. **Moral:** 22 "You shall not afflict any widow or orphan. 23 "If you afflict him at all, and if he does cry out to Me, I will surely hear his cry; 24 and My anger will be kindled, and I will kill you with the sword, and your wives shall become widows and your children fatherless. **Civil:** 25 "If you lend money to My people, to the poor among you, you are not to act as a creditor to him; you shall not charge him interest. 26 "If you ever take your neighbor's cloak as a pledge, you are to return it to him before the sun sets, 27 for

that is his only covering; it is his cloak for his body. What else shall he sleep in? And it shall come about that when he cries out to Me, I will hear him, for I am gracious. **Moral:** 28 "You shall not curse God, nor curse a ruler of your people. **Ceremonial:** 29 "You shall not delay the offering from your harvest and your vintage. The firstborn of your sons you shall give to Me.[6]

As such, it is impossible to distinguish between ceremonial, civil, and moral laws, and even if it were to be maintained, the fact that no one in Church history has sought to list every law beneath each label is a telling statement.[7] Yeshua's words in John 14:15 and other passages in Johannine literature regarding keeping the commandments must be understood as encompassing all relevant laws and applying to both redeemed Jews and Gentiles alike. John 10:16 further clarifies that the laws of Torah are not ethnocentric (for Jews only) but rather intended for all redeemed ethnicities. This point cannot be stressed enough

---

6 Tim Hegg, *Why We Keep Torah: 10 Persistent Questions* (Tacoma, WA: TorahResource, 2009), 135. He also goes on to show how the Sabbath can be understood as being all three.

7 Through the progressive revelation of YHWH, there appear to be three types of "Law." The first type of law are instructions that pertain to all believers. Believing Jews and Gentiles were the recipients (Matt. 5:19). The second type of law pertains solely to the Levites. A large portion of commandments are specifically for the tribe of Levi (Num. 1:50–51, 53; 3:5–10, 25–26, 31–32, 36–37; 4:1–33; 8:23–26; 18:1–6). Many of these relate to the Temple and priesthood, were operative in the past, and have been temporarily suspended until the establishment of the literal Millennium one day in the future (cf. Ezek. 43–46). The third type of law encompasses man-made rabbinical laws and the oral laws, which originate outside of Scripture. These legal ordinances appear to have emerged prior to the ministry of Yeshua (Matt. 15:1–9; 23:13–30; Mark 7:1–22) and were practiced by the Pharisees (e.g., Acts 15:5) but not documented until after the biblical record in the Talmud (comprising the Mishnah and Gemara).

according to the pronomian position, a theological reality affirmed by Daniel Block:

> It is evident from the New Testament that in the light of Christ, Christians do indeed have a new disposition toward the law. Not only do they see him as its fulfillment and through their union with him delight in its fulfillment themselves, but the law of God is written on Christians' hearts even as it was written on the hearts of true believers in the Old Testament. But we should not imagine that the law written on our hearts is different from the law revealed under the old covenant. Jesus said, "If you love me you will keep my commandments" (John 14:15), and "Whoever has my commandments and keeps them, he it is who loves me. And he who loves me will be loved by my Father, and I will love him and manifest myself to him" (14:21). In lifting these statements right out of Deuteronomy Jesus identifies himself with YHWH in the Old Testament. Furthermore, his use of the plural τὰς ἐντολάς μου, "my commandments," presupposes a specific body of laws with which the disciples are familiar. Here Jesus does not say generically and vaguely, "If you love me you will do as I say," as if this refers to marching orders for the future.[8]

Note the statement "we should not imagine that the law written on our hearts is different from the law revealed under the old covenant." While commentators will seemingly agree with this fact with regard

---

[8] Daniel I. Block, *The Gospel according to Moses: Theological and Ethical Reflections on the Book of Deuteronomy* (Eugene, OR: Cascade Books, 2012), 132. Block, at times, is extremely close to embracing a pro-Torah hermeneutic.

to the "moral" laws, they often don't apply this same reasoning with regard to the so-called "ceremonial" or "civil" laws. Such a position is insincere and inconsistent, as neither John, nor any other author of the Greek Scriptures, sees any such division. In fact, they understand all commandments to be embedded with morality.[9] Block is right in stating that the commandments, upheld by redeemed believers in previous generations as an act of love, remain just as true for redeemed believers—both Jew and Gentile—on this side of the Messiah's cross. Likewise, Roy Gane rightly notes the following:

> Good works of a converted Christian are not in opposition to faith; rather, the works result from faith. Belief and obedience work together, as shown by the functional parallelism in John 3:36: "Whoever believes in the Son has eternal life; whoever does not obey the Son shall not see life, but the wrath of God remains on him" (emphasis added). The gospel is to be believed (Mark 1:15; Acts 15:7; Rom. 1:16) and also obeyed (Rom. 10:16; 2 Thess. 1:8; 1 Pet. 4:17). Good works of a converted Christian are not in opposition to faith; rather, the works result from faith. Belief and obedience work together, as shown by the functional parallelism in John 3:36: "Whoever believes in the Son has eternal life; whoever does not obey the Son shall not see life, but the wrath of God remains on him"

---

9 "But what are his 'commands'? The parallels that tie together 'what I command' (v. 15, lit. 'my commands'), 'commands' (v. 21), and 'my teaching' (lit. 'my word' in v. 23, and 'my words' in v. 24) suggest to some that more is at stake than Jesus' ethical commands. What the one who loves Jesus will observe is not simply an array of discrete ethical injunctions, but the entire revelation from the Father, revelation holistically conceived (cf. 3:31–32; 12:47–49; 17:6)." D.A. Carson, *The Gospel According to John* (Grand Rapids: William B. Eerdmans, 1991), 448.

(emphasis added). The gospel is to be believed (Mark 1:15; Acts 15:7; Rom. 1:16) and also obeyed (Rom. 10:16; 2 Thess. 1:8; 1 Pet. 4:17).[10]

Berkowitz emphasizes that the Torah is not meant to be observed to attain justification before YHWH but rather serves to reveal human sinfulness, bring about YHWH's wrath, and act as a protector. Regarding the kingdoms of God and Satan, he writes that "[b]y the kindness, grace, and mercy of God, He has described for us exactly where the boundaries between these two opposite and diametrically opposed kingdoms lie [for t]hey are identified in the Torah."[11] He adds:

> Because the Torah tells us the truth—the difference between holy and unholy, clean and unclean, life and death—it is both a protection for us and a written revelation of the grace of God. Every man, woman or child who chooses not to live within the teachings of God, which produce life, is consigned to a place outside of the blessing and protection established by these teachings... [Furthermore, w]e can also tie in the description of the Torah as the national covenant and constitution... If we remain within the borders established by the teachings of Torah, we will enjoy our God-given inheritance and be protected from the influences of the idolatrous peoples arounds us. We will also serve as a light to those nations...this is also the reason that the "alien"...must live according to the

---

10 Roy E. Gane, *Old Testament Law for Christians: Original Context and Enduring Application* (Grand Rapids, MI: Baker Academic, 2017), 401.
11 Ariel and D'Vorah Berkowitz, *Torah Rediscovered*, 5th ed. (San Bernardino, CA: Shoreshim Publishing, 2012), 15–20.

Torah. For the sake of all those called to live [with]in...no act of rebellion can be allowed to compromise its holiness.[12]

Yeshua's commandments encompass the Torah and remain applicable to both redeemed Jews and Gentiles. The connection between love and commandment-keeping is consistent throughout Scripture, reinforcing that faith and obedience are inseparable. To suggest that some commandments are no longer relevant undermines the continuity of YHWH's Word, which remains binding and authoritative for all who seek to follow the Messiah.

---

[12] Ibid., 20–22.

CHAPTER 5
DOING THE COMMANDMENTS AS A COMMUNITY

In the beginning, when the history of humanity began with Adam, man was in fellowship with YHWH. Before Eve was created to physically help Adam, YHWH spiritually helped Adam and interacted with him. Adam was part of an established community the moment he existed. *He was the first human being to ever have contact with the Tri-Unity and was a part of a community prior to Eve.* All three persons of the one God fellowshipped with Adam. After this, he was joined by Eve, and the two fellowshipped with YHWH together and with one another. However, sin would soon manifest itself in the world, and from the moment it entered, it caused a barrier between the Creator and the creation that could be restored only by the death and resurrection of the sinless saviour, the promised Messiah. Bruce Demarest summarises:

> In the beginning, Adam was placed in the garden to enjoy friendship and communion with God. When the creature chose to assert his own autonomy rather than live under the Creator's gracious care, fellowship was broken. Hence Adam and Eve hid themselves from the Lord's presence (Gn 3:8). Yet God immediately sought them out (v 9) and revealed his plan for the ultimate restoration of sinners through the work of the Redeemer (v 15).[1]

---

[1] Bruce A. Demarest, "Fellowship," in *Baker Encyclopedia of the Bible* (Grand Rapids, MI.: Baker Book House, 1988), 789.

Some four thousand years after Adam, a man called John, son of Zebedee, became one of the original twelve disciples of Yeshua the Messiah. He was referred to as the "one whom Yeshua loved" and, along with his brother James, was amusingly titled the "sons of thunder." While often humble in those writings by his hand, rarely identifying himself as its author, it is apparent that this thunderous title was bestowed upon John because of his active nature during the ministry of Yeshua and thereafter. He was a disciple who was bold and uncompromising in his faith and did not care much for the closet Christian. Allegedly, the first book that John wrote was the Gospel of John. Its opening chapters mirror the opening scenes of Genesis referenced above. However, in this chapter, I want to focus on the second book he wrote, 1 John, one of four authored by the apostle, chronologically set after the events of his Gospel. In particular, I want to focus on one of the lesser known "one another's," so often cited throughout the Greek Scriptures. Among the more than fifty "one another" commands, some of which are repeated, fourteen come from the apostle John, with all but one emphasizing "love one another." Let us explore the other "one another," which focuses on *fellowship*:

> What was from the beginning, what we have heard, what we have seen with our eyes, what we have looked at and touched with our hands, concerning the Word of Life—and the life was manifested, and we have seen and testify and proclaim to you the eternal life, which was with the Father and was manifested to us—what we have seen and heard we proclaim to you also, so that you too may have fellowship with us [i.e. one another]; and indeed our fellowship is with the Father, and with His

Son Jesus Christ. These things we write, so that our joy may be made complete.
—1 John 1:1–4

In this chapter, it is my intention to focus on the last two verses. However, allow me to give some context first. Written sometime between 90–95 AD, the apostle John wrote 1 John specifically to Christians in churches established throughout Asia Minor. He starts the book by recalling the past, speaking not only of his own involvement with the "Word of Life"—Yeshua himself, as confirmed two verses later—but also referencing his earlier gospel and the book of Genesis through his use of the word "beginning." More so, he speaks of the Messiah's incarnation, his interaction with mankind, his teachings and his oneness with God the Father. It is in verses three and four, however, where we come across a startling revelation: because of what YHWH has done, the question is no longer *whether* we can be in a relationship with him, but rather the fact that *we already have one*. It is a done deal. Like Adam at the beginning of creation itself, we are now in fellowship with YHWH because of Yeshua. The apostle John writes, "you too may have fellowship with us; and indeed our fellowship is with the Father, and with his Son Jesus Christ." I wish to briefly explore the latter part of this sentence in order to fully grasp the former. Larry Oats writes the following regarding the word "fellowship":

> ["Fellowship"] is κοινωνία (*koinonia*); it refers to association for the purpose of mutual involvement. In the New Testament it routinely carries the idea of religious involvement. This is not the only term that speaks of the unity and fellowship among believers in the New Testament, but it is a significant term...The word can be used to refer to a sign of fellowship

or a proof of brotherly unity, such as a gift or contribution. The concept can also include activities that accompany the mutual interests. The definition of fellowship is important. "Fellowship" in the 21st century is a cup of coffee and piece of pie after the Sunday evening service. This is not the biblical concept of fellowship; biblical fellowship is partnership in ministry.[2]

Fellowship is a beautiful word, and while it first appeared in the Greek language over two thousand years ago, it only came into the English language in the twelfth century. If, however, I were to ask you what it means to have fellowship with YHWH, I wonder if you would have an answer that best captures its intended meaning. Fellowship with YHWH is not the same as fellowship with one another, though both are sweet to the soul. The fellowship spoken of here is not like that amongst brethren, but rather, directly with God as the product of your salvation. It is salvific in nature. What the apostle John is saying here is that YHWH *wants you to share your life with and in him willingly.* He wants to have communion with you like he had with Adam. Now saved and sealed, he wants you to fellowship with him. Secondly, he also wants you to have fellowship with his ecclesia, which you are now a part of. He is glorified by this order. As John 17:6 implies, God the Father gave you as a gift to Yeshua the Son, which resulted in your salvation. In turn, God the Father wants you to acknowledge who he is and what he has done for you, and walk with—not wrestle against—his Holy Spirit that is conforming you into the image of his Son according to his Torah. Fellowship with YHWH, then, is not only understanding

---

2 Larry R. Oats, "A Theology of Fellowship," *Maranatha Baptist Theological Journal* 4 no.1, 3–4.

that YHWH has saved you but that he wants you to know him as Father, as Son, and as Spirit. He wants you to know him intimately. You are to know all of him, and to know all of him is to love him; and to love him is to do his commandments. As Rekha Chennattu eloquently states:

> Jesus' covenant relationship with God manifested in Jesus' communion with, and fidelity to, the Father becomes a model for the disciples, who continue to reveal the glory of God by keeping the commandments (15:10). The community of the disciples is reminded of their covenant commitment to Yahweh or to the Father as an indispensable condition for discipleship and their status as the true vineyard. Keeping the commandments is an indispensable condition for abiding in Jesus' love (v.10) and for being friends of Jesus (v.14)." Both are conditional clauses.[3]

Ask yourself the following questions: do you fellowship with God the Father? Do you fellowship with God the Son? Do you fellowship with God the Spirit? Not just as Tri-Unity, but individually? Do you know how each has a different role in creation, your salvation, and in the end times? What I am saying here is that fellowship with YHWH must take place before fellowship with one another. How do you fellowship with each person of the Tri-Unity? You must study Scripture and find out not only what YHWH collectively does within his creation, but also the distinct roles of each of his persons. God the Father, the Son, and the Holy Spirit appear throughout all the Hebrew and

---

3 Rekha Chennattu, *Johannine Discipleship as a Covenant Relationship* (Peabody, MA: Hendrickson Publishers, 2006), 116.

Greek Scriptures. Each had a different role in creation, a different role in salvation, and a different role in the future. A practical way of fellowshipping with the persons of YHWH is learning about his different titles according to is persons; each member of the Tri-Unity has several throughout Scripture: Abba and El Shaddai, Son of Man and Lamb of God, Advocate and Restrainer. God the Father, God the Son, and God the Holy Spirit is to be fellowshipped with as one in three and three in one. A. W. Tozer, in chapter seven of his classic *The Pursuit of God*, encapsulates this well when he says the following:

> Private prayer should be practiced by every Christian. Long periods of Bible meditation will purify our gaze and direct it; church attendance will enlarge our outlook and increase our love for others. Service and work and activity; all are good and should be engaged in by every Christian. But at the bottom of all these things, giving meaning to them, will be the inward habit of beholding God. A new set of eyes (so to speak) will develop within us enabling us to be looking at God while our outward eyes are seeing the scenes of this passing world. Someone may fear that we are magnifying private religion out of all proportion... [Yet] Has it ever occurred to you that one hundred pianos all tuned to the same fork are automatically tuned to each other? They are of one accord by being tuned, not to each other, but to another standard to which each one must individually bow. So one hundred worshippers met together, each one looking away to Christ, are in heart nearer to each other than they could possibly be were they to become "unity" conscious and turn their eyes away from God to strive for closer fellowship. Social religion is perfected when private religion is purified. The body becomes stronger as its members

become healthier. The whole Church of God gains when the members that compose it begin to seek a better and a higher life.[4]

Once we know YHWH, we can make him known to others. The two great commandments of Mark 12:28–31 reinforce this order. They are a summary, not a substitution, of the laws of Torah. It is because of this fellowship with YHWH, the basis of our salvation, that we are able to fellowship with one another, the basis of our sanctification. Redeemed Jew and Gentile, brothers and sisters alike, are being conformed into the image of the Son, Messiah Yeshua. We partake in this glorious goal by fellowshipping with one another. As such, we return to our text: "what we have seen and heard we proclaim to you also, so that you too may have fellowship with us" (1 John 1:3). Let us explore this.

To live out the commandments effectively, a believer cannot be a lone sheep. YHWH intends for believers to be in a likeminded flock. This covenantal community, headed by the Chief Shepherd (John 10:14; 1 Pet. 5:4), is one ecclesia, the same people of YHWH since its conception at the foot of Mt. Sinai when the Torah was delivered to Moses. The Creator intended his creations to come together and to be conformed into the image of his Son, in accordance with his revealed will, preserved as the Torah. As Chennattu reminds us:

> The best way of expressing our love for God and keeping his commandments is by loving fellow humans…Sharing life with one's covenant partner is very essential to a covenant relationship. The life that the individuals hold is not private property, but something common, which has to be shared with others.

---

4 A. W. Tozer, *The Pursuit of God* (Harrisburg, PA: Christian Publications, 2008), 96–97.

In brief, keeping the commandments, loving and sharing with others, are intrinsic to the nature of covenant relationships.[5]

This was not a first century concept, but one that was ancient and intended for the ecclesia in the wake of its conception at Mt. Sinai:

> Grounded in the Lord's promise, "I will be with you" (e.g., Exod. 3:12, 16ff.), and governed and maintained by the covenant which was premised on that promise (e.g., Gen. 17:7–8; Josh. 24; Jer. 50:5), Israel enjoyed a unique relationship with Yahweh as the "people of God." Symbolic of God's presence with them were the cloud and the pillar of fire (Exod. 14:24; 40:34–38; Num. 9:15–23), the ark of the covenant (cf. Num. 10:35–36), and the tabernacle and temple (cf. Ps. 11:4; Ezek. 37:27). Although the Israelites were to accord special protection to strangers and foreigners who lived in their midst (Exod. 23:8; Deut. 10:18–19), they came to shun association with such heathen who were not among the chosen people (cf. Exod. 12:43; Neh. 9:2). To such a degree did the fellowship between God and his people determine the lives of the Israelites that the guilt of one who transgressed the covenantal stipulations extended beyond that person to his family and larger social units, and even to the entire nation of Israel (cf. Num. 16:31–32; Josh. 7:1; 2 Sam. 21:1–14; 24:10–17; 1 Chr. 21:12–17).[6]

---

[5] Rekha Chennattu, *Johannine Discipleship as a Covenant Relationship* (Peabody, MA: Hendrickson Publishers, 2006), 65.

[6] A. C. Myers, "Fellowship," in *The Eerdmans Bible Dictionary* (Grand Rapids, MI.: Eerdmans, 1987), 380.

We are commanded to fellowship with one another as a covenantal community. It's not an option. This does not mean, as some assume, merely gathering for casual conversation or going through the usual routine of weekly questions over coffee or tea. It does not mean a group of Christians getting together solely to see a film or sport game. It's so much more than that and is deeply embedded with love for another, which is no surprise coming from the apostle. It is an interdependent series of global relationships, dependent on YHWH. It is a living organism, a body with numerus parts (1 Cor. 12:12–26) and whose head is the Messiah Yeshua (Eph. 1:22–23).

F.E.L.L.O.W.

After reading numerous commentaries on the nature and application of fellowship, I have created an acronym to help believers understand and live it out: F.E.L.L.O.W. It stands for: *Family, Engaging, Loving, Learning, Only,* and *Walking.*

Family. In fellowship with one another, we are to understand that we are each a member of an eternal family, the household of God (Eph. 1:22–23). Galatians 4:5 says we have been adopted by YHWH, and Romans 9:8 says we are his children. Prior to the cross, Yeshua referred to believers as friends (John 15:15), but after his death and resurrection, he referred to them as brethren (Heb. 2:11). While I am not diminishing the place of earthly families by way of blood, we know that not all our friends and family will be saved, but ideally those in the ecclesia have been saved from sin into holiness. The person seated in your local congregation is an eternal family member by the Spirit—not by flesh and blood, which will one day pass away. Consequently, you will know them forever.[7] As for those in the ecclesia who have absent

---

7 This is explored in Joseph H. Hellerman, *When the Church Was a Family: Recapturing*

family members, believers are to fill that space with their presence, not as a substitute, but as a new source of love. How you love fellow believers shows how much you love your family, because the same heart that loves those within the walls of your home is the same heart for those within the walls of your congregation. Fellowship, in the first century ecclesia, was exampled in how they shared possessions; what was one Christian's was another Christian's because Christ gave it to them to begin with (Acts 2:44–45). That is how the contemporary ecclesia needs to be thinking and what it needs to return to.

Engage. Like groups on a high school campus, some believers like to congregate with familiar persons, as it if were a "holy huddle." While this is not necessarily bad, it is more secular than sacred. You may not be the same age, gender, ethnicity, or have the same interests or backgrounds as a fellow believer, but none of these are disqualifications from fellowshipping with one another. Your shared identity in Messiah Yeshua is enough, and that alone is sufficient to engage with others. Furthermore, you abide by the same commandments in loving him, according to his Torah. Furthermore, fellowship is not to be eclipsed by your privacy. This does not mean you must spend every second of the day with fellow believers, though as confronting as that sounds to some here on earth, it will be the norm in Heaven. Nor does it mean that believers should not have alone time with YHWH, for remember, even when you are alone with him, you are fellowshipping with the Tri-Unity. As fellowship is commanded and requires holy community, it is something you cannot do alone or with unbelievers. As Jensen rightly notes:

Jesus' Vision for Authentic Christian Community (Nashville, TN: B&H Academic, 2009).

For the people of God were not to fellowship with everybody. Indeed one of the characteristics of the nation Israel was its requirements of holiness that were to keep it separate from other peoples. They were to take no part in the religious expressions of other nations; they were not to intermarry with them or to adopt their practices morality or laws. They were to completely destroy and dispossess those who were already in the promised land – partly as a judgement of God on their sins and partly that the people and land of God were to be completely holy… Total inclusiveness of a tolerant relativism is completely at odds with Christianity. In his second letter to the Corinthians Paul asks a series of rhetorical questions that show the impossibility of unequal yoking (2 Corinthians 6:14–7:1)… So the scriptures urge, warn and command us to avoid certain people and fellowship. We are to have nothing to do with them. We must not help or give succour to them in their work. We are not to fellowship with them in eating and drinking. This is not a matter of personal preference or choice but of obedience to God's word. He commands us not to fellowship with them.[8]

I am not aware of any commentators who connect Yeshua's call for commandment observance in the Gospel of John with the fact that this Gospel contains the most commentary on the appointed festivals—*a perfect example of community engagement through obedience to the Torah.*

---

8   Phillip Jensen, "The Limits of Fellowship," Address given by the Dean of Sydney, Phillip Jensen, at the Sydney Lambeth Decision Briefing, Sydney, 14th March, 2008. https://phillipjensen.com/resources/the-limits-of-fellowship/. Jensen is inconsistent though, in contending that "within the New Testament there is a universality and inclusion that strikes a quite different note to the exclusiveness of Israel."

David deSilva at least admits, "The fourth Evangelist forges more explicit links between the events in Jesus' ministry (and Jesus' words) and Jewish festivals than any other New Testament author. The proximity of each particular festival casts a special, interpretative light on Jesus' actions and words, even as Jesus' actions and words show that the essence of the festival is captured in his person."[9] This is why Hebrews 10:25 is more likely a reference to engaging in festival observance and the importance of living out the commandments communally (in light of the epistle focusing on the Temple and its services).

Loving. The commandment of love in John 13:34 is the enlarged and renewed standard of love expected of the Messiah, a holy disposition first towards the Tri-Unity and then his ecclesia. In fellowship with one another, you must love your brother and sister in Messiah. Your love must be authentic, for not only do you love YHWH, the manifestation of love, but you are to love what he loves, which is the ecclesia. It is a love that is different yet equally important as the love you have for your earthly family, for it is founded in eternity and will be shared forever and ever. It is a love that has you smile when your brethren smile, frown when your brethren frown, and cry when your brethren cry. In 1 John 3:11–15, the disciple John appeals to Abel's righteousness and Cain's sin, both of which refer to the Torah before its codification at Mt. Sinai, and demonstrate the disposition of love a creature should and should not have before the Creator.

Learning. In fellowship with one another, you share the same Saviour, the same foundation. Knowing him and making him known is your commandment and commission in life. Learning about YHWH through his Scripture, whether it be husbands with wives, parents with

---

[9] David A. deSilva, *An Introduction to the New Testament: Contexts, Methods & Ministry Formation* (Downer Groves, IL: IVP Academic, 2004), 422.

children, between courting couples, among best friends, or in a Bible Study group, fellowship is learning all that you can about God the Father, God the Son, and God the Holy Spirit in order to grow in knowledge about him and share that knowledge with one another. As you learn about YHWH, spiritual maturity and healing take place and encouragement and hope abound. This is why we are commanded to read the Bible daily. We are to remember "you have known the sacred writings which are able to give you the wisdom that leads to salvation through faith which is in Christ Jesus. All Scripture is inspired by God and profitable for teaching, for reproof, for correction, for training in righteousness; so that the man of God may be adequate, equipped for every good work" (2 Tim. 3:15–17).

Only (with fellow believers). In fellowship with one another, one of the best ways to determine whether it is biblical or not, is that it can be done only with those saved by Messiah Yeshua. You cannot have biblical fellowship with an unbeliever. Fellowship as understood in Scripture is that which can be shared only with one whom you share an eternal foundation with. That foundation is YHWH, and it is paved by the commandments of the Torah. You can have coffee, dinner, and go out somewhere with *anyone*. Fellowship, however, must be Messiah-centred. Anytime brethren get together to share and talk about the Messiah or are in ministry, it is fellowship. Fellowship within congregations, fellowship with other congregations. Consider Acts 2:42–47:

> They were continually devoting themselves to the apostles' teaching and to fellowship, to the breaking of bread and to prayer. Everyone kept feeling a sense of awe; and many wonders and signs were taking place through the apostles. And all those who had believed were together and had all things in common; and they began selling their property and posses-

sions and were sharing them with all, as anyone might have need. Day by day continuing with one mind in the temple, and breaking bread from house to house, they were taking their meals together with gladness and sincerity of heart, praising God and having favor with all the people. And the Lord was adding to their number day by day those who were being saved.
—Acts 2:42–47

These verses are as comforting as they are radical. In focusing on the topic of fellowship, consider this: those who were fellowshipping with one another were once strangers, foreigners, even enemies. So it is the same today. Believers in the local congregation are different in that we are of different backgrounds, both ethnically, geographically, and for some, once morally and ethically. Messiah changed all that (Gal. 3:28–29). What unites believers in fellowship, in a way the world cannot understand, is our shared fellowship with Yeshua.

Walk. In fellowship with one another, you must walk alongside your brethren. Whether dancing together on the mountain on high or weeping together in the valley of darkness, you should either have brethren by your side or you should be next to your brethren. Fellowship means that because you have the Spirit of Messiah in you and are being conformed into his image, then wherever Messiah is on earth, you should be. His footsteps become yours. Obeying his commandments demonstrates your love for him. Yeshua is just as much in our coffee circles and Bible Study groups as he is in our cemeteries and hospitals. To walk by the side of your brethren can mean to simply be with them and saying nothing at all; it can mean being by their side and speaking words of wisdom or comfort. Walking with brethren is not just a few texts, emails, phone calls or a single visit; it's becoming their hands and feet when they can't walk or hold onto life. It's unceasing and sometimes not dependent on a response. Walking with brethren is understanding where they are at and meeting them on the path, not seeing them from a distant and remaining in your comfort zone. Likewise, the same mindset is true of the Christian who is in need of brethren to walk by their side; allow them to walk by your side. Pride and pity are powerless masters. When you pray for help, accept that it might be the hand of a brother in Messiah or the voice of a sister in him rather than God himself coming down from Heaven. Do not let the bitter weeds of disappointment by past brethren shun future brethren from walking by your side. Instead, cultivate the soil of fellowship so that restoration and new growth may take place. 1 John 2:6 is clear—we are to walk as Messiah Yeshua walked. He walked a path of Passover, not Easter. Omer, not Lent. Tabernacles, not Christmas. He ate clean food, not pork or shellfish. He congregated with believers on Sabbath at the end of the week, not the beginning. He witnessed the baptism of those able to confess faith, not the infants of believers. This was the way of Messiah and believers are to emulate him, not the ways created by men centuries after his earthly ministry. Rejecting God's commandments to uphold tradition was the way of the scribes and Pharisees, whom received the righteous anger of the Messiah for their burdensome joke. We are not to repeat the sins of those who walked in the wrong ways (e.g., Jer. 6:16, 7:23–24, 9:13, 10:23, 11:8).

In reflecting on this acronym, we see that fellowship is the strengthening of the collective ecclesia, local and universal, which together as one can do far more for YHWH and his kingdom than individually. His Torah, the constitution of the ecclesia, affirms this holy reality. Furthermore, several names for the ecclesia in Scripture enshrine this reality: the Body of Messiah (Eph. 5:22–23), the Flock of God (1 Pet. 5:2), the General Assembly and Church of the Firstborn (Heb. 12:23), and God's Field and Building (1 Cor. 3:9). When we think of the Great Commission of Matthew 28:16–20, Yeshua commands Christians to baptize unbelievers in the name of the Father, and of the Son, and of the Holy Spirit, and to obey all he has commanded. As such, we must teach and preach the God of Israel, raise up disciples within all cultures and generations according to the Torah which cannot be annulled, and undergo a ritual that does not save but shows obedience to YHWH and ushers their arrival into his family.

It is also worth mentioning that fellowship should never be taken for granted. Some believers, due to circumstances rather than choice, find themselves without fellowship. They are alone or know of no other believers where they live. They would love to have fellowship. In some countries, fellowship is a banned and an arrestable offence; if you are caught doing so, you are reported, arrested, tortured and imprisoned, like our brethren in North Korea. In Islamic countries, you can be executed under Muslim "Sharia" law for doing so. Fellowship leads to persecution for some believers in the world. Even here in the West, while we have not experienced persecution, oppression is mounting. In some Western countries, congregations and their members are discouraged by state laws and are now being fined and arrested for prayer. Never take fellowship for granted, as our eschatology teaches that tribulation is ahead.

Finally, in understanding and preparing our hearts to meditate on what fellowship with YHWH and one another means to us, the apostle John finishes off his revelation by highlighting the reward of these divine and earthly fellowships: *joy*. 1 John 1:4 says, "These things we write, so that our joy may be made complete." Fellowship with YHWH and one another is joyful. We are completed by God; his desire to be one with us and for us to be one with one another is a joyful truth and state of being.

How could it not? The word joy here, *chara* (χαρά), means "gladness," or better yet, "joy received from joy given." John's phrase "made complete" in these verses helps strengthen the understanding of joy expressed; it is a joy that cannot be born in the earth amongst man, it is Heaven-born and only YHWH can complete you. Joy according to Scripture, then, is based on who he is, what he has done for us, and what he has blessed us with. It is not to be confused with happiness, which is temporal and dependent on material possessions or other people, regardless of faith. Happiness is fleeting, much like physical food, but joy is eternal, like spiritual food. We can be joyful because of who God is and what he has done for us regardless of whether we "feel" joy. Joy here is based on truth, not emotions. Facts, not feelings.

In closing, consider the edifying words of Bridges' *True Community*, which is a great starting point to read more about fellowship. Note that the term communion used here as being about relationship between humanity and the divine:

> The vertical aspect of fellowship (union and communion with God) provides both the foundation and the pattern for the horizontal aspect (fellowship among believers). A community relationship among believers presupposes a living relationship with God and is, in fact, dependent on it. Where there is no vital union with Christ, there can be no sharing of the common life that believers have in Him. In the same manner, if believers are to share with one another in communion, they must first have something to share, something only obtained through communion with God… [T]he horizontal aspects of community [being] the sharing of the common life and the

sharing with one another that flows out of that life...[i]s all made possible by our vertical fellowship with God."[10]

Excursus: On the Doxological, Logocentric, and Pneumadynamic nature of the Ecclesia

In studying the foundations of ecclesial unity and purity in its identity, when we speak of its *doxological* nature, we are referring to its orientation of believers as they seek to glorify YHWH through their acts of worship. Who we are glorifying, how he desires to be glorified, and why we are glorifying him is evidenced through the worship we partake in and is not limited to our singing (Matt. 26:30; Eph. 5:19–20), but how we act, interact, think, and speak of him (cf. Eph. 1:3; 1 Tim. 3:16).

When we speak of its *logocentric* nature, we are speaking of a high view of bibliology and Christology. It is referring to Yeshua as the "Word of God" (John 1:1,14) a Christological term that focuses on Yeshua being the incarnation (albeit fulfillment) of everything spoken of in Scripture, and therefore, the incarnated *truth*. This is directly related to the concept of "logos," which expresses a statement, principle, or active word. Yeshua is logos in that he was the actuality of God's word(s); he is the truth of his power and glory. Scripture is also referred to as the "Word of God" (Luke 11:28). In this context, the emphasis on "logos" is different, as it is not talking of the person of Messiah Yeshua, but rather, what he embodied in what is known as the inspired Word of God, also known as the Torah.

When we speak of its *pneumadynamic* nature, we are referring to its assembling, empowering, and gifting by the Holy Spirit. Ephesians

---

10 Jerry Bridges, *True Community: The Biblical Practice of Koinonia* (Colardo Springs, CO: Navpress, 2012), 47–48.

1 teaches us that God the Father selected, Jesus Christ saved, and the Holy Spirit sealed believers that God predetermined to be saved before the foundations of the earth. Those that have been elected and called out from the nations are regenerated, indwelt, and sealed as convicted and confessed sinners (Rom. 8:9; Titus 3:5; Eph. 1:13–14), baptizing these believers into the "Church" (1 Cor. 12:12–14). The church, then, houses the Holy Spirit, and therefore, believers are dependent on him.

Straying from these three commitments leads to impurity, as to do so exposes a low or incomplete view of YHWH and his divine activities and roles, in addition to a false interpretation of the Scriptures and what they teach. Straying from YHWH and his Torah in these areas indicates a moving towards something which is not from YHWH, namely, self or a false idol. As such, this straying leads to disunity in that believers who remain true to God and his Word are being ignored and ridiculed by those who are ignorant, or worse, by false converts. YHWH desires us to be of the same mind (cf. Phil. 2:2), yet this unity must not be established in the absence of doctrine.

Among these three areas, the first a congregation is most likely to drift from is its logocentric nature. Far too many local congregations already have. The Scriptures have been ignored by countless so-called believers and have been attacked, discredited, or substituted with the ideologies and works of the world. This, I contend, extends to those churches that no longer see the Hebrew Scriptures as applicable or relevant. Countless church polls, denominational splits, and the clear state of the contemporary church affirm this.

What can a church leader do when such a threat emerges in the congregation? Teach and preach these truths, in and out of season (2 Tim. 4:2), regardless of the popularity of the message or the size of the congregation. A congregation that cultivates a love for reading and studying the Scriptures, the entire Torah, will cultivate their love for

God. Having a high view of God leads to a high view of his Word and its doctrines. Apathy, indifference, and false interpretations must be challenged, while practical applications and examples from ecclesial leadership should be provided for guidance and emulation.

CONCLUSION

[T]he Law is skilled in bringing home to its hearers by pastoral exhortation this turning of the heart to God in humility and love, gratitude and trust, and in making it fruitful for their understanding of the keeping of the law as a new attitude of the will. Again, by the derivation of the whole law from the command to love, the basic demand of the divine will for the surrender of the whole person to the divine Thou was brought within the comprehension of the simplest citizen. In this way even the commandment whose meaning is not immediately transparent—apart from the fact that it comes from the sovereign will of God, and is therefore valid as such—can still touch heart and conscience, because it derives from the counsel of the love of God, who has ordered all things for the sake of his people's salvation, and who accepts no keeping of the commandment just for the commandment's sake, desiring rather to see in each fulfilment of the law the living effect of a single-minded profession of love for God.[1]

Developing knowledge, understanding, and the skills necessary to read the Scriptures is an essential part of a Christian's faith practice. To read them in their historical setting, contextually consistent, then apply them in a contemporary manner is the goal of rightly diving the

---

1   Walther Eichrodt, *Theology of the Old Testament*, Vol. 2 (Philidelipha, PA: Westminster Press, 1967), 372.

word of YHWH. In analyzing the meanings of the words used in John 14:15, Christians can understand that Messiah Yeshua has called us to love him by abiding in the laws of Torah:

> How then can we fulfill our responsibility to love "more and more" [1 Thess. 4:10]? Recognizing that love is an inner disposition of the soul produced only by the Holy Spirit, what can we do to fulfill our responsibility?... the Spirit of God uses His Word to transform us. Therefore, if we want to grow in love, we must saturate our minds with Scriptures that describe love and show its importance to us. First Corinthians 13:1–3, for example, tells us of the emptiness of all knowledge, abilities, and zeal apart from love. First Corinthians 13:4–7 describes love in terms of specific attitudes and actions. Romans 13:8–10 describes love in fulfilling the law of God in our lives.[2]

The resistance to this divine prerogative is both concerning and inconsistent. It is concerning that YHWH's will is debated to the extent that much of what he commanded is deemed irrelevant to the modern ecclesia. This is despite claims from some that these commandments still hold value. It is inconsistent in that pastor-teachers and theologians alike insist that part of the Torah remains in full force, while the rest of it is no longer relevant. Estimates suggest around 300,000 federal statutes exist in the United States alone, and while not all are

---

2   Jerry Bridges, *The Fruitful Life* (Colorado Springs, CO: NavPress, 2006), 72. Though not a pronomian Christian, his statement should apply to all laws of the Torah. He later adds that prayer to the Holy Spirit to apply his Word and obedience ensures believers grow in love.

imposed on every citizen, the amount far eclipses those expected by YHWH in his Torah.

God is love (1 John 4:8,16), and his love, widely misunderstood by many, has long been a problem for some within and outside the ecclesia. From pastor-teachers to laymen, many Christians have declared the "unconditional love" of God, but in using this term (which does not exist in Scripture), those who have not accepted him as Lord and Saviour have often replied, "if he were a God of love, why does (insert any question)?" Clarification is needed. God's love is really "conditionally unconditional." What I mean is that no matter what you have done or how you have sinned, YHWH still loves you as an individual because his Son, Yeshua, died for all. YHWH "desires all men to be saved and to come to the knowledge of the truth" (1 Tim. 2:4; cf. Ezek. 18:23, 32). He is extremely pleased when individuals, in identifying their sin (the transgression of the Torah; Exod. 20:1–17; Deut. 5:6–21), repent and actively work to overcome it by abiding in his Torah. This love, however, *does not include one's sins* (Psalm 5:5, 11:5; Prov. 6:16–19). He hates sin and will punish those who choose to make sin lord in their lives over him as their Lord. The love of YHWH is *not* unconditional in the sense that he will just forgive humanity of everything, regardless of whether he is their Lord or Savior or whether they have confessed their sins or not. If you choose to willingly live in your sins, hating his commandments, then you do not have a relationship with YHWH.

Towards the end of the Gospel of John, the apostle captures a moment between Yeshua and the apostle Peter tying love and commandments together (John 21:15–17). After asking Peter if he loved him three times, while many commentators have been intrigued why the third question by Yeshua changes the type of love from *agapao* to *phileo*, few have taken the time to focus on the command to *bosko* (feed) and *poimano* (take care of) the sheep (i.e., flock of God). This

Conclusion

euphemism is referring to both pastoral teaching and pastoral care; orthodoxy and orthopraxy. Yeshua is expecting that those who will lead the local church—those shepherds under him—will teach them, and in accordance with the Great Commission (Matt. 28:16–20), his teachings include all he has taught the ecclesia from Mt. Sinia to his ascension. There is no reference, explicit or implied, that his commandments—the source of spiritual food and the compass by which care is administered—are to be compartmentalized or divided. In fulfilling, not abolishing, the Torah, Yeshua lovingly gifted his Bride with instructions to live a holy life until his return and to be set apart from the ways of the nations that have rejected his commandments. He declared that if we as believers love him, as wife to her husband, then we are to submit to his will and obey his sanctifying commandments born out of love. We do not reject Yeshua's commandments in hatred; instead, we love him by obeying them.

APPENDIX 1
THE ROLE OF GODLY WORKS IN THE MARKAN SHEMA

Though not often studied for its relationship to the Torah, the Gospel of Mark preserves countless examples of works demonstrated through practicing the Torah as an expression of love for YHWH (through Yeshua).[1] Every time a work is practiced by Yeshua or his disciples that is a direct response to a commandment (e.g., fasting, praying, Sabbath observance), what had been instructed in the Torah is physically evidenced. This dispels the argument that John 14:15 was only referencing those commandments instructed by Yeshua during his earthly ministry. Rather, it refers to the entire Torah as given and progressively enlarged since its codification at Mount Sinai. This is why Yeshua quoted from Deuteronomy in his spiritual battle with Satan (Mark 1:12–13; cf. Matt. 4:1–11). Using the Gospel of Mark, an uncommon work used to explore the role and impact of the Torah, one sees that Yeshua's declaration in John 14:15 can be demonstrated through all Gospel accounts. John stressed the importance of abiding in the commandments of YHWH through several of his writings (John 14:21, 23; 15:10; 1 John 2:3; 5:3; 2 John 1:6), yet this truth encompasses all biographical works of Yeshua and, by extension, his disciples. The truth of Yeshua's declaration, reiterated by John, must be mono-

---

1   I am entirely aware that this book is a study of John's Gospel and, as such, a brief study on Mark's Gospel seems out of place. My rational for including it is that I want to highlight that the relationship between love and the Torah—commandment observance being an affirmation of loving YHWH—is found consistently throughout Scripture, as attested in the Shema. John's contention paralleled that of the other Gospel authors.

lithic and evidenced throughout all the Greek Scriptures (cf. James 2:14–26). A powerful portion of Scripture on the direct correlation of practicing the commandments of YHWH and loving works is from Mark's citation of the "Great Commandment." The passage reads as follows:

> One of the scribes came and heard them arguing, and recognizing that He had answered them well, asked Him, "What commandment is the foremost of all?" Jesus answered, "The foremost is, 'Hear, O Israel! The Lord our God is one Lord; and you shall love the Lord your God with all your heart, and with all your soul, and with all your mind, and with all your strength.' The second is this, 'You shall love your neighbor as yourself.' There is no other commandment greater than these. The scribe said to Him, "Right, Teacher; You have truly stated that He is One, and there is no one else besides Him; and to love Him with all the heart and with all the understanding and with all the strength, and to love one's neighbor as himself, is much more than all burnt offerings and sacrifices."
> —Mark 12:28–33

This is a unique phrasing of the "Great Commandment" when compared to the other gospel versions (Matt. 22:37–40; Luke 10:25–28) in that it includes another descriptor of loving YHWH ("strength") and a direct connection to the Shema (Deut. 6:4), a culminative disposition of lovingly worshipping YHWH. MaGee also notes the connection between the Shema and the heart of the gospel when studying Paul's epistle to the Romans. He writes "that the Shema, the heart of the Mosaic Law, vindicates [Paul's] gospel, [and] is able to reject the charge (μή γένοιτο) that his gospel of faith undermines God's law."[2] The Shema, once heard, is intended to be acted out. MaGee's presupposition is that there is no tension between the codified laws by Moses (i.e., the Torah) and the gospel of YHWH of which Paul speaks; while different, they do not conflict and contradict, but rather harmonize and are in unity with one another. His focus on Paul's reinforcement of the Shema's teaching in Romans 3:30 is quite profound, for the proclamatory verse that proceeds it establishes the flawless conclusion: because YHWH is One, as taught in the Shema, which is representative of the entire Torah, then its laws are not nullified but established. In other words, because Romans 3:30 is true, being a text that represents the laws of Torah, then they are still active, practiced, and valuable. Likewise, the Gospel of Mark is highlighting that upholding the Shema, which represents YHWH's relationship with his people through his commandments, is the supreme evidence of loving him (exemplified in his Son, the "Word became flesh"; John 1:14). Le Peau infers this when he comments on Mark 12:33:

> *To love him with all your heart, with all your understanding and with all your strength, to love your neighbour as yourself is more important than all burnt offerings and sacrifices.* Some of the most stirring and well-known passages from Scripture surround this theme [Micah 6:6–8]...in addition, we read that obeying God (1 Sa 15:22; Jer 7:21–24; Hos 6:6–7), listening to God (Ps 40:6), repenting (Ps 51:16–17), stopping violence (Jeremiah 6:7, 20), not taxing the poor (Amos 5:11, 21–22, acting justly (Pr 21:3; Isa 1:11–17; Mic 6:6–8)—all these

---

[2] Gregory S. MaGee, "Paul's gospel, the Law, and God's Universal Reign in Romans 3:31," *Journal of the Evangelical Theological Society* 57, no. 2 (2014), 345.

supersede acts of worship. Not coincidentally, they are also all urgent, concrete ways of loving our neighbors (Mk 12:31).[3]

This is not to dismiss the place of offerings and sacrifices but rather to make clear the order of priority. Worship still matters and, in reality, work is a form of worship (Gen. 2:15). The point stressed here is that the works listed are all sourced from the Torah and were interwoven with the notion of love for both YHWH and those created in his image. Mark never attested the abolishment of the Law but in fact saw it as integral to the love a believer has for YHWH and fellow humans. Van Maaren notes, "throughout the narrative of Mark, law observance is an assumed part of righteousness…[and] correct understanding and practice of the law are both closely tied with membership in the kingdom of God… [Evidence of] the important role of correct understanding of the law is most clear when a scribe questions Jesus about the greatest commandment (ἐντολὴ πρώτη) in the law (12:28–34)."[4] McFarlane echoes these sentiments in seeing the "Markan narration is an exercise in seeking interpretive supremacy, both of the life and death of Jesus and of the Torah."[5] Hence the intertwined nature of Yeshua, the Word made flesh. Loving his commandments is loving him, for he "theópneustos" them. As Hiebert carefully notes:

> Love to God must possess the whole heart, the seat of personality, the whole soul, the self-conscious life, the whole mind,

---

[3] Andrew T. Le Peau, *Mark Through Old Testament Eyes: A Background and Application Commentary* (Grand Rapids, MI: Kregel Academic, 2017), 225.

[4] John R. Van Maaren, *The Gospel of Mark within Judaism: Reading the Gospel in Its Ethnic Landscape* (PhD diss., McMaster Divinity College, 2019), 299.

[5] Robert McFarlane, "The Gospel of Mark and Judaism," *Jewish-Christian Relations*, https://www.jcrelations.net/article/the-gospel-of-mark-and-judaism.html.

the rational faculties, and the whole strength, the entire active powers of man...If God is worthy of man's love, He must be loved with all of man's being...[and the second] command demands that he must exercise a love equal to that which he has for himself toward his neighbor.[6]

One should not read into these statements that Yeshua was making a distinction between imposed moral, civil, and ceremonial aspects of the Torah (which do not exist) or discarding two-thirds of them as is continually attested,[7] for in affirming the oneness of YHWH, he is affirming the oneness of the Torah. Love practiced toward a human "is much more" (Mark 12:33) than a practice that does not involve another human (i.e., sacrifices), but that is a differentiation of order, not equality. The holiness of YHWH has neither changed nor regressed with the progressive revelation of his commandments before the closing of the biblical canon.

This love in action is entirely consistent with the Hebrew worldview. It is essential to reframing the discussion of how one understands the direct correlation between works and love, to understand the differences between Greek and Hebrew worldviews. Though they wrote in Greek, the Gospel writers thought as Hebrews. They did not perceive the commandments of YHWH as theoretical, but rather they were to be actioned and worked out. In his pioneering study on the subject matter, Bowman writes that Hebrew "verbs especially, whose basic

---

[6] D. Edmond Hiebert, *The Gospel of Mark: An Expositional Commentary* (Greenville, SC: Bob Jones University Press, 1994), 352–53.

[7] For a prime example, see: William R. G. Loader, *Jesus' Attitude Towards the Law: A Study of the Gospels* (Grand Rapids, MI: W.B. Eerdmans Pub., 2002), 129–37 and R. L. Solberg, *Torahism: Are Christians Required to Keep the Law of Moses?* (Franklin, TN: Williamson College Press, 2022).

meaning always expresses a movement or an activity, reveal the dynamic variety of the Hebrews' thinking ... [w]hen a verb is to express a position like sitting or lying, it is done by a verb which can also designate a movement."[8] Hence, "motionless and fixed being is for the Hebrews a nonentity; it does not exist for them...Only 'being' which stands in inner relation with something active and moving is a reality to them."[9] In exploring the active nature of the Shema, Bowman further reveals that the Hebrew word "to be,"

> *hayah* contains a unity of 'being,' 'becoming,' and 'effecting,' that it dovetails neatly into the group of internally active (stative) verbs, and that it is best understood by us in the 'being' of an active person. If the essence of *hayah* best achieves expression in the being of a person, the next question involves this being's intrinsic value since this is determined by the subject. It is natural, then, to concentrate the inquiry upon the most important 'being' that the Israelite thought knows: the 'being' of its god, the universal author. It is to be recalled first of all that analytic judgements about God, as well as about other objects, that is judgements where for the Israelite that predicate inheres in the subject, are not expressed by *hayah* but by noun clauses.... 'Hear , O Israel Jahveh (is) our God, Jahveh (is) one' (Deut. 6.4)... It is characteristic of God's *hayah* that it seems to refer directly to the people's *hayah*:

---

[8] Thorleif Boman, *Hebrew Thought Compared with Greek* (New York, NY: W. W. Norton & Company, 1970), 28.
[9] Ibid., 31.

'Obey my command; thus I will be your God and you shall be my people' (Jer. 7.23; cf. 11.4).[10]

In citing the Shema, Mark was clearly aware of the physicality to one's relationship to YHWH. It was not merely a cognitive reaction to his commandments, but rather, an immediate response to work that affirmed one's love of YHWH. Schnittjer further adds that the "Torah freely interchanges 'you' singular and plural in its legal standards [and its] alternation of second person singular and plural pronouns affirms the interrelated collective and individual identity of God's people and spells out their associated collective and individual responsibilities."[11] Their works are the commandments of YHWH being lived out, both individually and collectively as an organic community of believers. In answering the rhetorical question as to why one performs godly works and how that cultivates a loving relationship with YHWH, he answers through demonstrating the direct relationship of one of his main commands:

> You collectively shall love the residing foreigner, because you collectively were residing foreigners in the land of Egypt (Deut 10:19). The context of Deuteronomy 10 emphasizes that Yahweh protects the vulnerable classes and loves residing foreigners and provides for their needs (v. 18). If Israel is called upon to collectively love the residing foreigner, they imitate Yahweh and become instruments of Yahweh's love by provid-

---

10   Boman, *Hebrew Thought Compared with Greek*, 47.
11   Gary Edward Schnittjer, "Say You, Say Ye: Individual and Collective Identity and Responsibility in Torah," *Center for Hebraic Thought* (March 9, 2022), https://hebraicthought.org/individual-collective-identity-responsibility-torah/.

ing for the hardships faced by the outsider. The responsibilities of Israel collectively to love the residing foreigner do not get satisfied by individual citizens caring for individual residing foreigners that they know personally (Lev 19:33a, 34b). Israel collectively needs to act as Yahweh does toward residing foreigners by proactively helping them with necessities (Deut 10:18–19). For all of this it would be a mistake to think that Deuteronomy is skewed toward collective social responsibilities.[12]

Here one sees love in action. It is working out the commanded instructions of YHWH. It is not an extrabiblical tradition or a man-made social gospel, but a triangular love between YHWH, the believer, and others. Hebraic worldview was one of action, not inaction, so faith is practical in its nature. This is attested throughout the gospels in which we see many works being the fulfillment of commands given throughout the Torah. Knowing YHWH and his Word comes with a charge to make him and his Word known.

---

12   Ibid.

APPENDIX 2
GOD IS LIGHT (1 JOHN 1:5–10)

Following the four Gospels, which recount the birth, life, death, and resurrection of Yeshua the Messiah, several of his apostles and disciples, directed by God the Holy Spirit (2 Tim. 3:16–17), wrote works that expounded on his teachings and preserved his ways, will, and words. In 1 John, the apostle John preserves what it means to have right orthodoxy and right orthopraxy; how to act, speak, and think as a Christian individually, among the brethren, and within a hostile secular world. 1 John is a practical primer of the Christian faith and most likely one of his final written works. While the book has often been touted as being a straightforward read in the English, in the original Greek, there has been countless debate as to the structure of John's book, of which there has not been universal consensus. Coombes seems to have theorised one of the most credible approaches, however, by observing the flow of words and literary structures throughout and noting "that the writer tends to convey ideas in small units rather than larger structures...convey[ing] one or two ideas in a few verses and would then convey a different (but usually related) idea in the next few verses," adding that sometimes "there is a three-fold repetition in the subunit, however one of the words is changed to its opposite...For example in 1:6–7 there is the pattern: *en tō skotei* / *en tō phōti* / *en tō phōti* ('in the dark'/'in the light'/'in the light')." He goes on to remark that in 1 John 1:6–2:2, the

> series of three paired antitheses. Each pair forms a subunit. While each subunit contains keywords which are repeated throughout the subunit (*en tō skotei* / *phōti; hamartia; hamar-*

tanō respectively) the rhetorical structure (*antithesis*) dominates the definition of the subunit, especially as the pattern of boasting followed by its counter positive statement is repeated three times through[out].[1]

While one cannot be dogmatic about this view, there is a validity based on the Greek. This is echoed by Jensen, who notes that 1 John contains a cyclical or spiral form argument and "should be understood as a dialectic discourse in which the author uses antithesis and dualism to convince the audience of the truth...[proposing] the following three-part structure: [Walking in the light – walking in darkness, works of righteousness – works of unrighteousness, Love produces life – hate produces death]," adding later that he "assumes a tripartite structure and then reads the text in light of his understanding of dialectic discourse, outlining the major dialectic themes (certainty, fellowship, the nature of YHWH, the opposition)...[and that these] themes link the sections together and tracing them reveals a dynamic argument that introduces a topic and then returns to it later developing it further."[2]

In 1 John 1:5, when utilizing various translations,[3] it is interesting to note the variations. In the original Greek,[4] the verse reads as follows:

---

1 Malcom Coombes, "A Different Approach to the Structure of 1 John," *Australian Catholic University* (n.d.): 6, 7, 8, 9. https://staff.acu.edu.au/__data/assets/pdf_file/0008/197648/Coombes_Structure_1John.pdf.
2 Matthew D. Jensen, "The Structure and Argument of 1 John: A Survey of Proposals," *Currents in Biblical Research* 12 no. 2 (2014): 196, 208–209.
3 This is to illustrate the point of the importance in choosing an accurate translation. I have chosen to compare 1 John 1:5–10 with the following three translations: NASB95 (New American Standard Bible; formal equivalent), CSB (Christian Standard Bible; functional equivalent), and CJB (Complete Jewish Bible; paraphrase). In reading the passage, there are some notable differences between the translations.
4 The 1881 Westcott-Hort New Testament (WHNU) will be consulted here.

και εστιν αυτη η αγγελια ην ακηκοαμεν απ αυτου και αναγγελλομεν υμιν οτι ο θεος φως εστιν και σκοτια ουκ εστιν εν αυτω ουδεμια. After opening the book, detailing his credentials as a reliable witness to life of Messiah Yeshua (cf. 1:1–4), John commences the first chapter by briefly surveying "the message" (synonymous with the gospel)[5] of Messiah and the response of a true believer. This announcement is in the present-tense according to the Greek. Hodges notes that "verse 5 clearly perpetuates the first-second-third person relationships so plainly visible in verses 1–4…The 'we' of course, both in verse 5 and 1–4, can only be an apostolic 'we' since the experiences claimed in verse 1 are such as were only enjoyed by those who had direct, personal contact with the Lord Jesus."[6] This point is echoed by Hegg as well, noting that the "Greek word order in this verse may well indicate an emphasis and this is because the word order in the Greek is different than John's normal style…by putting the stress on the verb 'to be,' 'to exist,' by placing it first in the sentence, John is telling us not only that this message is of utmost importance, but also that it has timeless significance."[7] When John says this *is* the message, by "adding the pronoun subject, following the verb, which had been moved to the fore of the clause, he is able to include the article with the predicate nominative 'message' without it being mistaken for the subject of the clause…[and by] this article with the noun, he alerts his readers that he is speaking of a specific and known message."[8]

---

[5] D. Edmond Hiebert, *The Epistles of John: An Expositional Commentary* (Greenville, SC: Bob Jones University Press, 1991), 56.

[6] Zane Clark Hodges, "Fellowship and Confession in 1 John 1:5–10," *Bibliotheca sacra* 129, no. 513 (2012): 48–49.

[7] Tim Hegg, *A Commentary on the Johannine Epistles: 1, 2, 3 John* (Tacoma, WA: TorahResource, 2018), 26.

[8] Gary W. Derickson, *1, 2 & 3 John: Evangelical Exegetical Commentary* (Bellingham, WA:

John goes on to speak of the nature of YHWH (Light) and that which is absent from him (darkness). The conflict and contrast between light and darkness were "widely prevalent in the Hellenistic conceptual world of John's day,"[9] though the Qumran community and the Dead Sea Scrolls speaks in such language. In this verse, in considering "Light" versus "light," the word φῶς (*phōs*) does not seem to indicate whether it favours one grammar over the other, however, as the context is metaphorical, it seems clear that the word should be in a capital, as it is referring to Christ (cf. Matt 4:16). The "articular noun 'God' is the subject; 'light,' without an article, is the predicate nominative; the two terms cannot be interchanged."[10] In stating this, it is worthwhile to note that "John is empathetic about this statement that "in Him there is no darkness at all," for he uses the double negative in the Greek."[11] MacArthur notes that the light spoken of in this verse is explained in a Hebrew parallelism from Psalm 36:9.[12] The three translations consulted do not differ greatly in this verse, other than the NASB95 capitalising the word light and the NASB95 and CJB overemphasising there is no darkness in YHWH ("at all" and "none"; οὐδείς), which the NASB95 gets correct. This is because it is translated as a direct quotation rather than indirect.[13]

    Lexham Press, 2014), 81.

9   Zane Clark Hodges, "Fellowship and confession in 1 John 1:5–10," *Bibliotheca sacra* 129, no. 513 (2012): 50.

10   D. Edmond Hiebert, *The Epistles of John: An Expositional Commentary* (Greenville, SC: Bob Jones University Press, 1991), 57.

11   Tim Hegg, *A Commentary on the Johannine Epistles: 1, 2, 3 John* (Tacoma, WA: TorahResource, 2018), 31

12   John MacArthur, *1–3 John*, The MacArthur New Testament Commentary (Chicago, IL: Intervarsity Press, 2007), 24.

13   Gary W. Derickson, *1, 2 & 3 John: Evangelical Exegetical Commentary* (Bellingham, WA: Lexham Press, 2014), 78.

1 John 1:6 reads as follows: εαν ειπωμεν οτι κοινωνιαν εχομεν μετ αυτου και εν τω σκοτει περιπατωμεν ψευδομεθα και ου ποιουμεν την αληθειαν. John proceeds to make a definitive statement that if one is in communion with YHWH and yet willingly sins, they are untruthful with their nature. The "Greek verbs in the first phrase... are both present tense...[and] would indicate that John intends us to understand these as a pattern of life."[14] The "articular designation 'in the darkness,' placed emphatically forward, marks the actual sphere of conduct as antithetical to the nature of God."[15] The three translations consulted differ more in this verse in that there is variation in the translation of ποιέω (*poiéō*), in which the NASB95 renders it *practise* (past tense in the Greek) and the CJB renders it *living*. The common translations for the word are "make" or "do." The CSB renders the open statement as a rhetorical question, which is not inferred in the Greek, though the "form of the Greek conditional clause rendered if we say is one which expresses a contingency that is, at least theoretically, capable of realization."[16] If one is truly saved, as John is, what he proposes is impossible, though had it not been for YHWH, it would be possible. To "lie and... not practice the truth" is in the first-person plural form of the present tense verb, and by doing so, includes him.

1 John 1:7 reads as follows: εαν δε εν τω φωτι περιπατωμεν ως αυτος εστιν εν τω φωτι κοινωνιαν εχομεν μετ αλληλων και το αιμα ιησου του υιου αυτου καθαριζει ημας απο πασης αμαρτιας. John highlights that the shared nature of the believer who is truly in communion with YHWH ensures communion with others whom are

---

14 Ibid., 33.
15 D. Edmond Hiebert, *The Epistles of John: An Expositional Commentary* (Greenville, SC: Bob Jones University Press, 1991), 60.
16 Zane Clark Hodges, "Fellowship and confession in 1 John 1:5–10," *Bibliotheca sacra* 129, no. 513 (2012): 51.

with YHWH. The "point is simple: if we walk where he is (in Greek the pronoun he is emphatic), then we and he both have something in common that we are sharing."[17] As YHWH "Himself is in the Light," the phrase contains "a comparative conjunction, to complete the protasis draws a comparison between the believer and God."[18] John goes on to acknowledge the blood of Yeshua and its power over sin, to which the CJB translation renders the name of Jesus to the Hebraic name Yeshua and καθαρίζω (*katharízō*) as "purifies," which, while not wrong, is more often translated into cleanses (as in the other two translations). As a present tense verb is used here, the cleansing spoken of here is ongoing, and while it took place at a point in history, its affect is perpetual.[19]

1 John 1:8 reads as follows: εαν ειπωμεν οτι αμαρτιαν ουκ εχομεν εαυτους πλανωμεν και η αληθεια ουκ εστιν εν ημιν. John says that those who declare sinlessness are deceiving themselves and are without truth. This deception is emphasised in the Greek, as the "reflexive pronoun [is] the object of the verb, placed emphatically forward, stress[ing] that the resultant deception is our own doing."[20] John's take on sin here is interesting. The "anarthrous noun αμαρτιαν is a qualitive rather than indefinite noun because of the verb 'to have,' when followed by an abstract noun such as αμαρτια, indicates a 'general quality'…[therefore] John is looking at sin as a principle rather than a specific act."[21] The three translations consulted are generally uniform

---

17 Ibid, 53.
18 Gary W. Derickson, *1, 2 & 3 John: Evangelical Exegetical Commentary* (Bellingham, WA: Lexham Press, 2014), 100.
19 D. Edmond Hiebert, *The Epistles of John: An Expositional Commentary* (Greenville, SC: Bob Jones University Press, 1991), 63.
20 Ibid, 65.
21 Gary W. Derickson, *1, 2 & 3 John: Evangelical Exegetical Commentary* (Bellingham, WA:

in translation, though the CSB again renders the opening statement as a rhetorical question even though the Greek does not infer it.

1 John 1:9 reads as follows: εαν ομολογωμεν τας αμαρτιας ημων πιστος εστιν και δικαιος ινα αφη ημιν τας αμαρτιας και καθαριση ημας απο πασης αδικιας. John makes clear that in confessing to sin, YHWH is faithful to his word, and as he is righteous (and his righteousness has been imputed to us as believers in his sacrificial death), will cleanse us from all unrighteousness. Hegg notes that the "opening conditional clause...is a third class conditional in the Greek...[and] this type of construction aims to emphasise the real and true nature of the outcome."[22] This is assured through the holy characteristics exhibited by one who is a true believer. Verses six to nine are structured in such a way to reveal that they parallel each other in a Semitic style (A-B-A-B).[23] The CJB's rendering of ὁμολογέω (*homologéō*) as "acknowledge" is far too narrow a translation and is better rendered as "confess" as it is in the NASB95 and CSB. To acknowledge something does not infer one will naturally confess it. This is again true when the CJB chooses "trustworthy and just" for πιστός (*pistós*) and δίκαιος (*díkaios*), yet these are not common translations, as the usual is "faithful and righteous." While similar, there are differences that could lead to theological variances. This challenge is emphasised more so in the last part of the verse by some scholars, as the "Greek of this phrase is difficult to translate into English, and the reason is because the verbs "to forgive"... and "to cleanse"...are both in the aorist tense, which may well give the sense of "forgiving" and purifying" once and for all,"[24] and thus,

---

Lexham Press, 2014), 104.
22 Tim Hegg, *A Commentary on the Johannine Epistles: 1, 2, 3 John* (Tacoma, WA: TorahResource, 2018), 37.
23 Ibid.
24 Ibid, 39.

absolve the need to continually confess and ask for forgiveness as a believer. A believer can express their gratefulness as a part of their spiritual discipline. Also noteworthy is that the "our" in the opening verses has been added and is not present in the Greek manuscript.

1 John 1:10 reads as follows: εαν ειπωμεν οτι ουχ ημαρτηκαμεν ψευστην ποιουμεν αυτον και ο λογος αυτου ουκ εστιν εν ημιν. John ends the chapter by repeating the principle of verse eight, but now, having laid the foundation of communion with YHWH in v. 7, he declares that those believers who claim to be without sin are not just deceiving themselves but making YHWH a liar and thus invalidating their right to think of themselves as saved. Here, the "perfect tense, 'have not sinned,' asserts a past condition of sinlessness which continues up to the present moment."[25] This time, like the CSB before it, the CJB translation poses the statement as a rhetorical question, yet the Greek does not infer that. The NASB95 and CJB translations render ἁμαρτάνω (*hamartánō*) as "sinned" as to establish something that has been done in the past (and therefore ongoing), whereas the CSB speaks of "sinning" in the present. The former translation seems to better fit the context of the verse. The CJB places the word "Word" with a capital letter which could confuse one theologically as that could refer to either the Scriptures themselves or Yeshua himself. That is not implied in the NASB95 and CSB translations. Λόγος (*logos*) used here is contextualized by the prior verse, which is speaking about the importance of language and words as opposed to the *logos* of YHWH spoken of in John 1.[26]

---

25   D. Edmond Hiebert, *The Epistles of John: An Expositional Commentary* (Greenville, SC: Bob Jones University Press, 1991), 68.
26   Ibid., 69.

While delivering practical advance, encouragement, and warnings to believers and non-believers alike, 1 John contains grammar, structure, and words that are unique. For centuries, scholars have debated the structure of the book, appealing to methods ranging from thematic analysis, source criticism, literary criticism, linguistic analysis, to appeal to ancient rhetorical practices, in addition theories as to the argument of the book: "there is no developed argument, there is an association of ideas, there is a cyclical or spiral form argument, it is parallel to John's Gospel, [or] it is chiastic."[27] Regardless of one's position on these matters, one is still able to understand the original meaning of the text contextually, grammatically, and historically, as one reads through and interprets the Greek. The most accurate translations are those that are closest to the original manuscripts (i.e., word-to-word), and in surveying the NASB95, CSB, and CJB, it is the first of these that best captures the intended meaning and rendition of what was penned by John the apostle, by guidance of God the Holy Spirit, two millennia ago.

---

27 Matthew D. Jensen, "The Structure and Argument of 1 John: A Survey of Proposals," *Currents in Biblical Research* 12 no. 2 (2014): 196, 207.

APPENDIX 3
THE GOSPEL OF MESSIAH YESHUA

What is the Gospel?

The gospel is the free and good news of salvation that was secured through the incarnational birth, righteous life, sacrificial death, physical resurrection, witnessed ascension, and ongoing intercession of the Lord Yeshua Messiah; he lovingly drew us towards him, forgave and cleansed us of our death-bound sins that once separated us from God, and now indwells us with his Holy Spirit, which is conforming us into his image for the glory of YHWH.

The Gospel then is Love.

What do I mean by it being love? Well, YHWH, who is the embodiment of *love*, who, in his *loving*kindness, *lovingly* created, saved, and shared himself with his creations, and because he *loved* us so much, he *lovingly* sacrificed himself to free us of our unloving and hateful sin to secure eternity with us. He loves us so much he was willing to share the love he as a Tri-Unity experienced before the creation of the universe with you and me—and will continue to do so with those he has elected forever and ever.

The Gospel is love. YHWH is love.

This takes us to the moment in the gospels in which Yeshua is asked one of the most important questions during his ministry: Matthew 22:37–40. There, unloving sinners asked Yeshua, the incarnation of love itself, the following question: what is the greatest commandment?

Yeshua replied: "To love the Lord your God with all your heart, mind, and soul." In Mark's gospel, the word "strength" is added.

Yeshua continues: "And love your neighbour as yourself."

This is a huge commandment. Radical. Confronting. Challenging. Impossible. Yet, it is the greatest commandment according to Yeshua, God in the flesh. Love YHWH, love others. Know YHWH, make him known to others.

An impossible commandment to fulfil, one might ask?

Well... yes and no.

First, the "yes." It is impossible to love YHWH if you have not accepted the gospel. You cannot love YHWH if you have not accepted the gospel of the Lord Yeshua Messiah. It is impossible. You can never do it. Never. You could spend a lifetime studying Yeshua, and you would still not be able to love him with all your heart, mind, soul, and strength. If you went to church every weekend, but never accepted the gospel of the Messiah, then all the singing, praying, and listening to Scripture being preached will not make you able to love YHWH. If you don't believe me, just ask Judas. He was close to the gospel, walked alongside the gospel, felt its salvific warmth, but never accepted it. It is impossible to love YHWH in the absence of accepting the gospel. It's impossible to escape the second death of Hell without hearing and believing the gospel.

Let me make this clear: the gospel of Messiah Yeshua is a gospel of love—divine love gifted, and mortal love willingly returned. The only way you can love YHWH then is if you have accepted the gospel of Yeshua, the very One who has become your identity.

This leads us to the "no" when asked whether it is impossible to fulfil the commandment of Matthew 22:37–40.

It is not impossible to love YHWH *if you have accepted the gospel.* You *can* love YHWH if you have accepted the gospel of the Yeshua the Messiah. It is possible. It is joyful. In fact, it is natural. You can do nothing else. If you have accepted the gospel, you have accepted Yeshua. If you have accepted Yeshua, you have accepted the triune nature of YHWH. If you have accepted this profound mystery, you have accepted his gift of love—a love that has set you free and a love that is easily returned to him and shared with others so that they may know of God's love, a love that is perfectly depicted in the gospel.

Unbeliever, *hear me*...the gospel saves! It is love beyond comprehension. Do not fool yourself and think you can love YHWH without the gospel. Equally foolish is to pronounce that you have accepted the gospel, yet have not yet come to love him with all your heart, mind, soul, and strength! No such separation exists. One is the other! Waste no time...*love the gospel and love God, for each breath you take without confessing this is a breath of hatred and a breath closer to eternal separation from YHWH*! Make today the day of salvation; yesterday you were ignorant about the gospel, but now you have no excuse. Tomorrow is not assured.

Believer, *hear me*...the gospel has saved you! Messiah Yeshua is your Lord and Saviour! Rejoice again in the day of your salvation. Continue to deepen and broaden your love for YHWH with all your heart, mind, soul, and strength and use your breath to thank Yeshua. Be grateful for the gospel you accepted and use that same breath to share the gospel with family, friends, and strangers alike. Share the good news before you receive the bad news that they did not hear the gospel you were called to deliver.

POSTSCRIPT

This is by no means an exhaustive study on the relationship between love and the commandments instructed by Messiah Yeshua. It is intended to be a starting point and a call for consistency when exegeting the Scriptures. It is my prayer that this excursion into John 14:15 has both challenged and comforted your understanding of the relationship between loving YHWH and abiding in all his commandments, as defined by Scripture, not denomination. It was an honor to contribute to this series of "Pocket Guide" books and to further pronomianism as a pro-Torah hermeneutic in the field of biblical scholarship.

If you are interested in seeing more of my work, please follow me at https://the2ndreformationwithdrszumskyj.substack.com.

BIBLIOGRAPHY

Alexander, T. Desmond. *From Paradise to the Promised Land: An Introduction to the Pentateuch.* Grand Rapids, MI: Baker Academic, 2012.

Barrs, Jerram. *Delighting in the Law of the Lord: God's Alternative to Legalism and Moralism.* Wheaton, IL: Crossway, 2013.

Bauckham, Richard. "For Whom Were Gospels Written?" *The Gospels for All Christians: Rethinking the Gospel Audiences.* Edited by Richard Bauckham. Grand Rapids, MI: William B. Eerdmans Publishing Company, 1998.

Berkowitz, Ariel and D'Vorah. *Torah Rediscovered*, 5th ed. San Bernardino, CA: Shoreshim Publishing, 2012.

Block, Daniel I. *The Gospel according to Moses: Theological and Ethical Reflections on the Book of Deuteronomy.* Eugene, OR: Cascade Books, 2012

Bock, Darrell L. *Studying the Historical Jesus: A Guide to Sources and Methods.* Grand Rapids, MI: Baker Book House Company, 2002.

Boman, Thorleif. *Hebrew Thought Compared with Greek.* New York, NY: W. W. Norton & Company, 1970.

Bridges, Jerry. *True Community: The Biblical Practice of Koinonia.* Colardo Springs, CO: Navpress, 2012.

———. *The Fruitful Life.* Colorado Springs, CO: NavPress, 2006.

Brumbach, Joshua. *John's Three Letters on Hope, Love and Covenant Fidelity: A Messianic Commentary.* Clarksville, MD: Lederer Books, 2019.

Bruner, Frederick Dale. *The Gospel of John: A Commentary.* Grand Rapids, MI: William B. Eerdmans, 2012.

Carson D.A. and Douglas J. Moo. *An Introduction to the New Testament.* Grand Rapids, MI: Zondervan, 2005.

———. *The Gospel According to John.* Grand Rapids, MI: William B. Eerdmans, 1991.

Chennattu, Rekha. *Johannine Discipleship as a Covenant Relationship.* Peabody, MA: Hendrickson Publishers, 2006.

Coombes, Malcom. "A Different Approach to the Structure of 1 John." *Australian Catholic University.* https://staff.acu.edu.au/__data/assets/pdf_file/0008/197648/Coombes_Structure_1John.pdf.

Demarest, Bruce A. "Fellowship." *Baker Encyclopedia of the Bible.* Grand Rapids, MI: Baker Book House, 1988.

Derickson, Gary W. *1, 2 & 3 John: Evangelical Exegetical Commentary.* Bellingham, WA: Lexham Press, 2014.

deSilva, David A. *An Introduction to the New Testament: Contexts, Methods & Ministry Formation.* Downer Groves, IL: IVP Academic, 2004.

Eichrodt, Walther. *Theology of the Old Testament.* Volume 2. Philadelphia, PA: Westminster Press, 1967.

Furnish, Victor Paul. *The Love Command in the New Testament.* London, UK: SCM Press, 1973.

Gane, Roy E. *Old Testament Law for Christians: Original Context and Enduring Application.* Grand Rapids, MI: Baker Academic, 2017.

Grayston, Kenneth. *The Gospel of John: Epworth Commentaries.* London, UK: Epworth Press, 1990.

Harrison, Everett F. "John." *The Wycliffe Bible Commentary.* Edited by Charles F. Pfeiffer & Everett F. Harrison. Chicago, IL: Moody Publishers, 1990.

Hegg, Tim. *A Commentary on the Johannine Epistles: 1, 2, 3 John.* Tacoma, WA: TorahResource, 2018.

———. The "Great Commission: How Yeshua Defines Taking God's Light into the World. Tacoma, WA: TorahResource, 2016.

———. Why We Keep Torah: 10 Persistent Questions. Tacoma, WA: TorahResource, 2009.

Heibert, D. Edmond. *The Gospel of Mark: An Expositional Commentary* (Greenville, SC: Bob Jones University Press, 1994.

———. *An Introduction to the New Testament: Three Volume Collection*. Waynesboro, GA: Gabriel Publishing, 2003.

———. *The Epistles of John: An Expositional Commentary*. Greenville, SC: Bob Jones University Press, 1991.

Hellerman, Joseph H. *When the Church Was a Family: Recapturing Jesus' Vision for Authentic Christian Community*. Nashville, TN: B&H Academic, 2009.

Hengel, Martin. *The Four Gospels and the One Gospel of Jesus Christ*. Translated by J. Bowden; London: SCM Press, 2000.

Hodges, Zane Clark. "Fellowship and confession in 1 John 1:5–10." *Bibliotheca sacra* 129, no. 513 (2012): 48–60.

Ironside, H. A. *John*. Grand Rapids, MI: Kregel Publications, 2006.

Issler, Klaus. "Jesus' Example: Prototype of the Dependent, Spirit-Filled Life." *Jesus in Trinitarian Perspective: An Intermediate Christology*. Edited by Fred Sanders and Klause Issler. Nashville, TN: B&H Publishing Group, 2007.

Jensen, Matthew D. "The Structure and Argument of 1 John: A Survey of Proposals." *Currents in Biblical Research* 12 no. 2 (2014): 194–215.

Jensen, Phillip. "The Limits of Fellowship." Address given by the Dean of Sydney, Phillip Jensen, at the Sydney Lambeth Decision Briefing, Sydney, 14th March, 2008. https://phillipjensen.com/resources/the-limits-of-fellowship/.

Jobes, Karen H. *John: Through Old Testament Eyes*. Grand Rapids, MI: Kregel Academic, 2021.

Johnson, Thomas F. *1, 2 & 3 John – Understanding the Bible Commentary Series*. Grand Rapids, MI: Baker Books, 1993.

Keener, Craig S. *The Gospel of John: 2 Volumes*. Grand Rapids, MI: Baker Academic, 2010.

Köstenberger Andreas J. & David Crowther, "Leading with Love: Leadership in the Johannine Epistles." *Biblical Leadership: Theology for the Everyday Leader*. Edited by Benjamin K. Forrest, Chet Roden. Grand Rapids, MI: Kregel Publications, 2017.

Kruse, Colin G. *The Letters of John*. The Pillar New Testament Commentary. Grand Rapids, MI: William B. Eerdmans, 2000.

Laney, J. Carl. *John*. Moody Gospel Commentary. Chicago, IL: Moody Publishers, 1992.

Le Peau, Andrew T. *Mark Through Old Testament Eyes*. A Background and Application Commentary. Grand Rapids, MI: Kregel Academic, 2017.

Limbeck, M. "ἐντολή." *Exegetical Dictionary of the New Testament*. Volume 1. Edited by Horst Balz and Gerhard Schneider. Grand Rapids, MI: William B. Eerdmans Publishing, 1990.

Loader, William. *The Johannine Epistles*. Epworth Commentaries. London, UK: Epworth Press, 1992.

———. *Jesus' Attitude Towards the Law: A Study of the Gospels*. Grand Rapids, MI: W.B. Eerdmans Pub., 2002.

MacArthur, John. *John: 12–21*. The MacArthur New Testament Commentary. Chicago, IL: Intervarsity Press, 2008.

———. *1–3 John*. The MacArthur New Testament Commentary. Chicago, IL: Intervarsity Press, 2007.

MacDonald, William. *Believer's Bible Commentary*. Nashville, TN: Thomas Nelson, 1995.

MaGee, Gregory S. "Paul's gospel, the Law, and God's Universal Reign in Romans 3:31," *Journal of the Evangelical Theological Society* 57, no. 2 (2014).

McFarlane, Robert. "The Gospel of Mark and Judaism," *Jewish-Christian Relations*, https://www.jcrelations.net/article/the-gospel-of-mark-and-judaism.html.

Morris, Leon. *Testaments of Love: A Study of Love in the Bible*. Grand Rapids, MI: William B. Eerdmans, 1981.

Mounce, William D. ed. "Love." *Mounce's Complete Expositor Dictionary of Old & New Testament Words*. Grand Rapids, MI: Zondervan, 2006.

Myers, A. C. "Fellowship." *The Eerdmans Bible Dictionary*. Grand Rapids, MI.: Eerdmans, 1987.

Oats, Larry R. "A Theology of Fellowship." *Maranatha Baptist Theological Journal* 4 no.1: 3–4.

Pigeon, E. Richard. *AMG's Comprehensive Dictionary of New Testament Words*. Chattanooga, TN: AMG Publishers, 2014.

Renn, Stephen D. ed. "Commandment." *Expository Dictionary of Bible Words*. Peabody, MA: Hendrickson Publishers, 2005.

Reuschling, Wyndy Corbin. *Reviving Evangelical Ethics: The Promises and Pitfalls of Classic Models of Morality*. Grand Rapids, MI: Brazos Press, 2008.

Richards, Lawrence O. "Command/Commandments." *Expository Dictionary of Bible Words*. Grand Rapids, MI: Zondervan, 1985.

Riesenfeld, H. *"tēreō* [to watch over, [protect]." *Theological Dictionary of the New Testament: Abridged in One Volume*. Grand Rapids, MI: Wm. B. Eerdmans, 1985.

Ryle, J. C. *John*. Volume 3: Expository Thoughts on the Gospels. Edinburgh, UK: The Banner of Truth Trust, 2012.

Sánchez, Juan. "What Did Jesus Do?" *The Gospel Coalition* (October 2012). https://www.thegospelcoalition.org/article/what-did-jesus-do/.

Schneider, "ἀγάπη." *Exegetical Dictionary of the New Testament.* Volume 1. Edited by Horst Balz and G. Gerhard Schneider. Grand Rapids, MI: William B. Eerdmans Publishing, 1990.

Schnittjer, Gary Edward. "Say You, Say Ye: Individual and Collective Identity and Responsibility in Torah." *Center for Hebraic Thought* (March 9, 2022). https://hebraicthought.org/individual-collective-identity-responsibility-torah/.

Schrenk, G. "Commandment." *Theological Dictionary of the New Testament: Abridged in One Volume.* Edited by Geoffrey W. Bromiley. Grand Rapids, MI: Wm. B. Eerdmans, 1985.

Solberg, R. L. *Torahism: Are Christians Required to Keep the Law of Moses?* Franklin, TN: Williamson College Press, 2022.

Stern, David H. *Jewish New Testament Commentary.* Clarksville, TN: Jewish New Testament Publications, 1992.

Strecker, Georg. *The Johannine Letters.* Translated by Linda M. Maloney. Edited by Haold W. Attridge. Minneapolis, MN: Fortress Press, 1996.

Szumskyj, Benjamin. *The Laws of Torah in the Sanctification of the Modern Christian: A Brief Introduction to Pronomianism.* Wilmington, DE: Vernon Press, 2026.

Tozer, A. W. *The Pursuit of God.* Harrisburg, PA: Christian Publications, 2008.

Van Maaren, John R. *The Gospel of Mark within Judaism: Reading the Gospel in its Ethnic Landscape* (2019). ProQuest Dissertations and Theses Global, https://macsphere.mcmaster.ca/bitstream/11375/24581/2/Van_Maaren_John_R_finalsubmission2019June_PhD.pdf.

Vine, W. E. "Agape." *Vine's Expository Dictionary of Old & New Testament Words*. Nashville: Thomas Nelson Publishers, 1997.

Wheaton, D. H. "Love." *Evangelical Dictionary of Theology*. Edited by Walter A. Elwell. Grand Rapids, MI: Baker Academic, 2001.

Wilber, David. *How Jesus Fulfilled the Law: A Pronomian Pocket Guide to Matthew 5:17–20*. Clover, SC: Pronomian Publishing, 2024.

Zodhiates, Spiros. *The Complete Word Study Dictionary: New Testament*. Iowa Falls, IA: World Bible Publishers, 1992.

———. "ἐντολή entolē." *The Complete Word Study Dictionary: New Testament*. Iowa Falls, IA: World Bible Publishers, 1992.

www.ingramcontent.com/pod-product-compliance
Lightning Source LLC
Chambersburg PA
CBHW060331050426
42449CB00011B/2727